BARE BONES CHILDREN'S SERVICES

Tips for Public Library Generalists

Anitra T. Steele

Association for Library Service to Children

AMERICAN LIBRARY ASSOCIATION
Chicago and London   2001

While extensive effort has gone into ensuring the reliability of information appearing in this book, the publisher makes no warranty, express or implied, on the accuracy or reliability of the information, and does not assume and hereby disclaims any liability to any person for any loss or damage caused by errors or omissions in this publication.

Text and cover design by Dianne M. Rooney

Composition by ALA Editions in AvantGarde and Bodoni Book using QuarkXpress 4.1 for the PC

Printed on 50-pound white offset, a pH-neutral stock and bound in 10-point coated cover stock by Batson Printing

The paper used in this publication meets the minimum requirements of American National Standard for Information Sciences—Permanence of Paper for Printed Library Materials, ANSI Z39.48-1992. ∞

Library of Congress Cataloging-in-Publication Data
Steele, Anitra T.
    Bare bones children's services : tips for public library generalists / Anitra T. Steele [and] Association for Library Service to Children.
       p.   cm.
    Includes bibliographical references and index.
    ISBN 0-8389-0791-1 (alk. paper)
      1. Children's libraries—United States. 2. Public libraries—United States. 3. Children's librarians—United States. I. Association for Library Service to Children. II. Title.
    Z718.2.U6 S74 2001
    027.62'5—dc21   00-048492

Printed in the United States of America

05 04 03 02 01   5 4 3 2 1

CONTENTS

PREFACE

Some people are "naturals" at the job they are doing, some people make themselves successful in their fields, and some people are thrust into positions they never thought to have. This book was written for that third group. It presupposes some knowledge and background in basic librarianship and the willingness, if not the training, to extend quality library service to that segment of the population that is fourteen years old and younger.

Providing library service to children may seem overwhelming to someone unexpectedly placed into that position. Although it is not necessarily difficult, it does require a certain level of knowledge and a sensitivity to children. This book was written as a guide and reality check for those taking on the assignment. It aspires to provide the specific information in a practical summary that a person needs to serve children well.

In library school I had not planned to be a children's librarian. I took no children's literature or programming classes. I hadn't taken any child development or early education classes as an undergraduate. I was going to be an adult services librarian. But when I graduated, children's librarian positions were all that were available. I parlayed my background as an avid reader and my experience as a babysitter into my first job as Young People's Librarian at the Livingston County Memorial Library in Chillicothe, Missouri. Because I was the first to hold that job, I was not faced with the "but we always do it this way" model. Being able to develop the job in my own way had a positive effect on me. I hope the readers of this book will also benefit from doing things their own way.

In the book I have tried to include things I wish I had had access to when just starting out. For example, public speaking is often the most frightening aspect of children's librarianship and the one least likely to be shared with other departments (very few catalogers or reference librarians are asked to speak to mother's clubs about tracking down that elusive tracing or obscure answer). Therefore, I have included outlines, samples, and examples of the kinds of programs and presentations a children's librarian may be asked to do. You will find an outline for the typical "Sharing Books with Your Children" talk, storytelling and book talking tips. Some of the philosophy underpinning library service to children and how service to children differs from service to the general adult population are also discussed here.

I wrote this book because I wanted to encourage others to become children's librarians. One of the proudest moments of my life came when a former latchkey child I had befriended at my first job looked me up at a library conference and thanked me for inspiring her to become a librarian. Very few jobs can offer this type of reward and far-reaching impact.

Throughout the text, I refer to specific books that cover this book's topics in more depth rather than try to duplicate that information. After all, this book is just the bare bones of what you need.

ANITRA STEELE
Children's Specialist
Mid-Continent Public Library

Introduction
Qualities of Effective Children's Librarians

A quick glance at the library employment classifieds will give you an idea of what a children's librarian is supposed to be able to do. The requested skills seem to fall within the abilities detailed in ALSC's Competencies:

knowledge of the client group

skill in administration and management

ability to communicate

knowledge of the collection

ability to present programs

advocate for children

be an active self-learner

There are also, however, frequently desired qualities that are different from the ability to manage a department and collection.

Library administrators seek children's librarians who are enthusiastic about children, books, and reading. Administrators know that this enthusiasm transmits itself to those the children's librarian comes in contact with. It also fosters creativity and resourcefulness among the staff, and interest and support from the public.

Specific programming abilities are also requested in the classifieds. Administrators ask for children's librarians who are experienced in storytelling, puppetry, art, music, and theater.

Historically, some libraries rigorously trained their children's staff to present programs. More commonly today, potential staff members are expected to bring at least some skills with them or to avail themselves of the opportunity to learn them through workshops and in-service classes.

Librarians fill an increasing number of job roles. While they have been trained to be information providers and collection developers, the Internet has affected the sources of that information and the look of the collection. It has also changed how librarians communicate and learn. Librarians can take advantage of distance learning opportunities and share ideas and concerns with others in faraway places using the Internet. Changing social policy reinforces the need to be an advocate, collaborator, and partner, and because we are still librarians we continue to facilitate learning, advise readers, and manage libraries.

I like it when parents bring infants to my programs. I see it as job security.

Effective children's librarians are enthusiastic, energetic, flexible, and resourceful. They have mastered the competencies and continue to learn. They can tell stories to preschoolers, speak to parent groups, and help find that tricky answer. They communicate clearly on all levels, work cooperatively within and out of the library, and advocate for children and quality library service for them.

Know Your Clientele

1

Understanding how children develop and grow helps you plan activities and select materials that are appropriate. This knowledge can also reinforce your patience with storytime children or preteen program participants.

Theories of Child Development

Children's librarians, like any professional working with children, should be aware of theories of child development.

The most recent theories concern early brain development. These findings encourage new parents to enrich their infants' environment and to spend time engaging them with music and language. Reading and using the library fit in well with the results of these studies. What parents, librarians, and educators have known instinctively has now been confirmed by neuroscience. Brain imaging technologies allow the growth of the human brain to be measured and mapped. The images reveal that the human brain is not fully developed at birth—the brains of infants and young children are much more active and complex than once thought. Experiences like hearing books, rhymes, and music; seeing pictures; and touching and smelling books actually help develop brain cells, or neurons, as well as connections, or synapses, between brain cells. Early exposure to books and other library activities can literally have a lifetime effect.

Classic child development theories are also important. Erik Erikson, influenced by Freud, believed people pass through eight stages in their lives. Four of Erikson's stages occur in childhood: early childhood—achieving autonomy; middle childhood—developing initiative; late childhood—becoming industrious; and adolescence—establishing identity.

Abraham Maslow described a hierarchy of needs. According to Maslow's theory, people have five basic needs: physiological, including the need for food, shelter, clothing; safety; belongingness and love; esteem; and self-actualization. Beyond these five basic needs are cognitive and aesthetic needs. According to this hierarchy, all children have the need for physical well-being, the need to love and be loved, the need to belong, the need to achieve competence, the need to know, and the need for beauty and order.

The behaviorists, including John Watson, B. F. Skinner, and Albert Bandura, believed that children learn to behave through positive and negative reinforcement and punishment. These theories are behind techniques that encourage children to behave or learn for praise and prizes, not because they are expected to or for the intrinsic pleasure and reward of learning.

Jean Piaget's development levels are based on four kinds of operations: assimilation, accommodation, conservation, and reversibility. For example, a child learning something new first assimilates it into what she already knows. She then accommodates the new material with the known material for understanding. Conservation deals with the child's perception of appearance and reality. Reversibility allows her to accept that although appearances may be deceiving, they don't alter the basic reality of the situation. Piaget's four major stages of development, based on these operations, are

sensorimotor intelligence (from birth to age two, or the appearance of language)

pre-operational thought (the preconceptual phase, from age two to four, when behavior is based on subjective judgement; and the intuitive phase, from age four to seven, when the child is better able to use language to describe mental activities and to generalize what he or she experiences)

concrete operations (from age seven to eleven, when the child can use logic to reason out problems and to deal with concrete experiences and things)

formal operations (after age eleven, when the young person is able to think beyond immediate experience and to theorize)

Children from Birth to Three

Libraries are offering more services for the very young child. Board book collections and special toddler time and lapsit programs are commonplace. You can reassure parents that the library has materials for their newest family member and that infancy is not too young to start developing the library habit.

A good way to introduce parents to the library's materials and programs is with a parent collection. A parent collection includes books from both the adult collection and the children's collection and is kept in the children's room. This collection can provide parents with helpful information on how their children develop, how to address specific issues that arise during different developmental periods, and how to use books and other library resources from birth on with their children. You can also include community information in the parenting collection. For example, a schedule of parent education classes about discipline issues or a flyer about an author of a child development book who will be speaking at the library would be helpful.

Judith Shoot, Livingston County Library (Chillicothe, Missouri), sends new parents a card entitling them to a Baby Time Capsule. The capsule is a decorated plastic ice cream bucket that contains a list of suggestions for the time capsule contents, coupons, a bibliography of parenting books, a board book, a program schedule, and of course, a library card application.

Recommend Mother Goose rhymes, children's songbooks, and books of fingerplays and bounces to new parents. Consider including an activity or fingerplay learning program, which is a nice way to bring the children's book collection to life for parents, who may have forgotten most rhymes and fingerplays.

Encourage parents to recite rhymes and sing to their little ones. The babies love the sounds and rhythm and will learn to differentiate voices and assimilate the vocabulary in these rhymes. Accent the beat with clapping to help the baby develop her own sense of rhythm. Let parents know that these "value added" activities encourage brain development as well as parent-child bonding.

Judy Nichols at the Wichita (Kansas) Public Library developed a program called "Pattycakes" where she leads young families through many different rhymes and bounces, demonstrating them on a large doll. Parents follow along with their children and leave the session with a booklet of the rhymes and bounces they have just learned.

Suggest to parents that they use old magazines or catalogs for page turning, which very young children enjoy. Encourage parents to point out pictures in the magazines to their little ones and to talk about what is happening in them. Children seem especially interested in pictures of other babies.

As children become toddlers, encourage board books and simple story reading for them. Look for clear, simple pictures that are easy to "read," stories that reflect the child's own world, and tales that parents won't mind reading over and over.

Children from Three to Five

Preschool children begin to show definite likes and dislikes. While they continue to like the familiar, they are also beginning to develop a sense of humor. Books that mirror home, like *Goodnight Moon* by Margaret Brown, or show the ridiculous, like Shaw's *Sheep in a Jeep*, find favor with this age group. The rhythms and appealing sounds of words can attract children to books again and again.

Concept books about counting, shapes, and the alphabet work well with this age group as do wordless picture books that invite the child to tell his own story. Short children's poetry is appropriate as are classic children's books. Some books continue to resonate with today's children, such as *Make Way for Ducklings*, *Where the Wild Things Are*, and *Mike Mulligan and His Steam Shovel*.

When you suggest folk and fairy tales to parents, be sure to mention that these stories have many versions. The parents should check the story's ending to be sure they are comfortable with it.

You can also bring in appropriate easy nonfiction at this point. There are some exciting series illustrated with full-color photographs as well as simple math and science concept books created especially for young children.

Children from Six to Nine

Children in the early elementary grades are learning and practicing reading. They need books to help them become fluent readers. Books that are written for children who are learning to read without help are called *easy readers* or *beginning readers*. Beginning readers use a simple vocabulary, large print, and short sentences, and they use pictures to help the reader figure out the meaning of words. They have a specific appearance in terms of the size of the book and the number of words on a line. Many beginning readers indicate the reading level on their covers. While this indication is helpful, don't overly rely on it—children's interest in a book's subject can have a profound effect on their ability to read it.

Reading interests of this age group become more diverse. While they still like to be read aloud to, they start asking for scary stories or joke books that they can read on their own. They move from beginning readers to "chapter books" (easy novels divided into chapters, around 64 pages long with some illustrations, that appeal to second and third graders) to longer juvenile fiction and nonfiction.

The transition from picture books to juvenile fiction and nonfiction can be difficult for some children. The denser print, fewer pictures, and thicker size can intimidate a struggling reader. When suggesting books for this age, try to offer both beginning readers and easier juvenile fiction and nonfiction. If the child really wants a "grown-up" book but her skills are not up to it, you can suggest joke books, trivia, or poetry. These books come in the "grown-up" format but offer manageable amounts of print on each page. They are also designed to be dipped into, which can be a plus for a slow or unsure reader, rather than to be read from beginning to end.

Eight- and nine-year-olds also start showing interest in juvenile series books. Series trends come and go, and whether you purchase them may depend on your library's collection development policy. Series books encourage reading for pleasure at a time when required reading may be a challenge but when practice is crucial. They also engender a feeling of accomplishment in young readers and confidence in their reading skills.

Children from Ten to Fourteen

If your library defines "child" as up to age fourteen, then ten- to fourteen-year-olds are the big kids around the children's library. They may feel the children's area doesn't have anything to offer them. You can suggest books to them, or you can create a separate area that features books for this age group that help them view life through another's eyes or provide them with information that can improve their own lives. Perhaps you can provide group opportunities for them to read and discuss some favorite books and thereby hone their critical skills.

A special display area can convince older children that the children's area still has lots to offer them. They will feel like they're selecting books that were chosen especially for them! Fill a shelf or table—as far away from the "baby" books and easy readers as possible—with books of high interest to preadolescents and adolescents. Include science and health books from both the children's and adult collection that will interest the ten- to fourteen-year-old. Don't forget a range of fiction, from mysteries to humorous books. Use this area to promote library and community activities for this age group, too.

Some children in this age group may also be eager to help in the library and will enjoy assisting you. You can enlist their assistance and help build their sense of responsibility. Perhaps they can select books to recommend to younger children, or cut out shapes for an upcoming preschool program.

Many states have children's choice book award programs to encourage children in this age range to read more widely. In a typical program, a committee of librarians (usually school librarians) develops a list of nominees published in the preceding year. Children who read a required number of these nominees then vote for their favorites. If your library supports this type of program, read the nominees yourself so that you can make recommendations to inquiring children.

Parents

Parents who come into the children's area are often need-driven. They may need a book about potty training or some material to take on vacation with their four-year-old. Showing them how the area is laid out and where special materials can be found is often all you need to do. Sometimes, though, additional questioning about what parents are looking for is warranted. The father looking for Mark Twain books for his fourth grader may want books nominated for the Mark Twain Book Award, not necessarily only those by Samuel Clemens.

You should also encourage parents to help their children at the library's computer terminals. They can "surf the 'Net" together and use software the library has available. Not only are these shared activities enjoyable for the parents and children, they also help reinforce the range of material the library has available.

Parents should be encouraged to stay in the children's area with their children and help them select books. Of course, you should make it clear to the parents that you are available if they need help. Parents must also be made aware that they should never leave small children unattended in the children's area. The library is a public place, and staff members do not necessarily know who should be with a child.

Childcare Providers

A good relationship between childcare providers and the library is a winning combination. Providers who use the library for unit materials and bring their charges to library programs are enriching the lives of the children in their care. Consider offering "Special for Childcare" programs or materials in quantity "to go." If staffing allows, offer to provide programs at childcare centers or licensed childcare homes to alleviate transporting small children.

Something Special for the Childcare Provider

Some libraries provide kits designed for the early childhood eductor. These early learning kits typically include:

    books for the young child

    lists of related books

    resources for the adult, such as relevant web sites

    washable puppets and other educational toys

    educational games

    handouts about the library for the childcare provider
        to send home.

Teachers

Teachers use the public library for several reasons, including curriculum support and student resources. Sometimes they request multiple copies or subject collections. Library policy determines if these services can be provided. A good relationship with teachers can encourage them to give you timely alerts about upcoming special assignments and cooperative projects.

One way to foster a good relationship with teachers is to offer a teacher assistance program. With this program teachers can request topics, using the Teacher Assistance Form shown here. The library then gathers collections of materials on their requested topics and makes the collections available for the teacher to check out, for the students to check out, or for the students to use in the library. To make this program work, you may need to request interlibrary loan materials. You will also need to have an understanding with the teacher about handling renewals and late or lost fees.

Keeping good records of teacher assistance program requests and the collections developed to meet them will make this service easier to provide over time. You can also use the requests as a collection development guide.

Keep in mind that a public library has a different mission than a school library. The public library serves a broader clientele, and cannot be expected to provide everything a school library would.

Special Groups

Children's librarians work with a variety of special groups in different ways.

Homeschooled children using the library collection like a school library often need a wider variety of resource materials than children completing traditional school assignments. They can form a nucleus of a young people's book discussion group or a useful, informal review group. Families homeschool their children for different reasons, and those reasons should be respected.

Children with special needs or disabilities should be welcomed to programs, and accommodation must be made for them. Include the handicap-accessible symbol on all program and promotional material. Have interpreters available for signing during programs when hearing-impaired children may be in attendance. Is there a magnifier on a catalog terminal in the children's area for vision-impaired children? Purchase at least a few juvenile fiction titles in large print and know what they are. Also learn what

Sample Teacher Assistance Form

Please return or fax this form two to four weeks before the assignment date so that we may obtain materials from other sources if necessary.

Library name:

Phone number: Fax number:

Today's date: Date(s) materials are needed:

Topic:_____

(include a copy of the assignment, if possible)

Teacher(s):   Home Phone:

School: Phone:

Library card number: Fax:

Best time to contact with questions:

Type(s) of material needed: Fiction____   Non-Fiction____

                    Pamphlets____   Videos (if copyright allows)____

How many items will be required?   Number of students:

Are pictures more important than text?

Check the service you would like us to provide:

_____ SUPPLEMENTAL CLASSROOM COLLECTION   A collection of materials on a given topic to supplement a teacher's or the school library's collection. The teacher will check these items out and will use them in the classroom only. The teacher will be responsible for all materials checked out. A maximum of four copies of any one title will be provided.

_____ STUDENTS' CHECK OUT COLLECTION   A collection of materials on a given topic that will be kept at the public library. The library staff will gather these items and house them in a specific location in the library. Students may then check these items out on their own library cards.

_____ RESERVE COLLECTION   A collection of books on a given topic that will be kept at the public library. Items in this collection will be considered reference and may not be checked out by the students. Reserve Collection service works best when there are not many sources available on a particular topic.

If you have specific titles in mind, please attach a list.

We may not be able to provide large quantities of books on seasonal topics, such as Valentine's Day and Thanksgiving.

COMMENTS:

other state or regional resources are available to augment your materials and programs for children who are blind or physically or learning disabled. Maintain a file of interpreters and application forms for your State Library for the Blind and Physically Handicapped.

Ask parents of children with special needs what would make the library more accessible and accommodating for their children. Sometimes they can recommend easily made changes that help all concerned. Consider inviting students from your local state school for children with disabilities to library events or making it a stop on your story telling rounds. Pet shows, magicians, puppet shows, visits by police search and rescue dogs, and other standard children's programming are enjoyed by all children.

Your library's clientele includes children who are gifted readers as well as reluctant readers. Gifted readers need books that are challenging to them but that are still within their emotional and experiential grasp—for example, six-year-olds who read at the sixth grade level need books that are longer and more difficult but that deal with events and ideas within their reach. Reluctant readers also need books within their emotional and experiential grasp that easier to read but are not perceived as "baby" books— for example, sixth graders who read at a lower reading level still want appealing and appropriate books that they can read with little help. Consider providing lists for each group that take their needs into consideration. There may be existing lists that are appropriate, or you can work with a teacher to develop them. And don't forget to ask young readers who are gifted or reluctant to recommend titles!

An international study on reading ability discovered that Finnish children were the best readers in spite of the many hours of television they watched. It seems that popular American and British TV programs are not dubbed but rather close-captioned!

Organized large groups of children (such as day camps and visiting classrooms) are a special clientele in that serving them effectively requires advance scheduling and preparation. Advance notice of the visit, information on what is wanted, and clarification on checking out materials, student use of the Internet, photocopying, and so on should be provided by the group's director to make the experience more effective and pleasant. Consider scheduling separate, repeat performances and programs for children in groups, especially where their presence at an open-to-the-public event could overwhelm the others in attendance. These special performances would also allow you to tailor activities and supplies specifically for the group—for example, the materials for a craft project could be packaged in advance to send back with the group's director rather than completing the project in the library.

2

Services

Services available to children using the library are some of the more visible parts of the children's librarian's job. These services include reference, readers' advisory, and homework support. Reference is defined as any service aimed at helping children and others access information. Readers' advisory service is helping children and others find materials of interest. Homework support is exactly what it sounds like.

Reference

Good reference service to children varies very little from good reference service to adults. The two basic components are the same: people skills and professional expertise. Many of the reference resources—the library's catalog and online databases, almanacs, dictionaries, and encyclopedias—are also the same for both children and adults.

Good reference service to children differs only slightly in approach and communication. Come out from behind the reference desk to approach children who appear to need help. Inquire if they are finding everything they need. If a child is working on a homework assignment, ask to see it so you know exactly what the teacher has assigned. Ask where the child has already looked and suggest other search strategies or subject headings. Be sure that you talk to the child, not the accompanying parent.

If a child's question is sufficiently complex to require a more formal reference interview, tailor your interview. Does a preschooler who asks for "Barney" books want fiction titles or informational books about real dinosaurs? An older child's question for information may be for a term paper or for casual interest. How many formats of the information are needed, and how many sources? Where has the student already looked and under what headings?

Share information with the child as you ask these questions and make suggestions. Let her know what kinds of answers are best found in what sources, whether in a book, a periodical, the encyclopedia, an almanac, or an online database. If time allows, work with the child to locate the information. If it doesn't, at least start her in the right direction, and follow up later to see if she has found materials or information. Offer to place holds for materials in circulation or at another location. As with adults, complete your assistance by asking, "Does this completely answer your question?" to give the child a final opportunity to get what she needs.

When providing reference service to children, it is especially important to take their requests seriously and respond to them in the order they come in. You should be approachable and friendly but also professional and helpful. Model how to use a library by helping the child search the databases and book stacks, which is much more effective than lecturing on how to use the library.

In addition to standard library reference materials, professional resources for children's materials are very helpful, especially when you are looking for appropriate materials for the very young. These sources include *Best Books for Children, Children's Catalog, A to Zoo,* and *The Elementary School Library Collection.* These books give brief annotations, age designations, and indexes, and they can direct you (and the child) to an appropriate book where a simple shelf or catalog scan may not. They are also useful references for parents, teachers, and other adults interested in children's books.

Online Reference

Just as the toddler banging on a keyboard isn't really typing, young people who don't know how to develop or implement a search strategy are not really searching the Internet. Internet searching skills need to be taught like all library use skills. Young searchers should be around eight years old, to have the necessary spelling and thinking skills.

Children's librarians are working to provide programs that will introduce children to newer technologies. Spend time with the child-friendly search engines, like Yahooligans (http://www.yahooligans.com). See what web sites they pull up for general questions and how they approach topics. Add good sites to your files to save future search time. Keep a continually updated file of useful child-appropriate Web addresses handy to save search and surf time.

Approach the Internet positively. Stress to young people the positive aspects of it as well as appropriate and safe Internet etiquette. Emphasize that there are "bad" sites, but there are more good ones, and if a "bad" one comes up, young readers should quickly move on. Post computer use rules near the equipment.

Go over Internet search tips with children and help them define and refine what they are looking for before they go online, to save time and increase the likelihood of success.

Internet Search Tips

Although all search engines work a bit differently, use the following examples to explain search strategies.

1. Words separated by spaces are treated as an *exact phrase search*. Only sites or documents that contain this exact phrase will be returned. This level of search is the most precise and will result in the fewest number of hits.

   emperor penguin = "emperor penguin"
   Mark Twain Award = "mark twain award"

2. Words and phrases separated by commas are treated as an *OR search*. Sites or documents containing any of the specified search terms will be found. This level of searching is the least precise and will result in the greatest number of hits.

   emperor, penguin = emperor OR penguin
   Mark Twain, Award = mark twain OR award

3. Words and phrases separated with *and* are treated as an *AND search*. Sites or documents containing all the terms specified, in any order of place within the site or document, will be returned. This level of searching is a good balance between the exact phrase search and the OR search.

   emperor AND penguin = emperor AND penguin
   Mark Twain AND Award = "mark twain" AND award

4. All searches are *case insensitive*. Use of upper or lower case letters will not affect the result.

> Mark Twain Award = mark twain award

While answers found on the Web may seem more authoritative and advanced for frequently occurring student questions, traditional sources are usually faster and more reliable to search. Increasingly, reference services must include evaluating whether online resources are more appropriate than print resources as well as how to evaluate a web site's accuracy and authenticity.

The demand to use the library's computers may need monitoring to be sure they are available to all.

You may want to develop a sign-up sheet to help ensure that the computers are available to all. The sign-up sheet shown here as a sample would be kept at the children's desk. Children write their names on the sheet, and staff members monitor the time spent at the computer and the library's software.

Computer Sign-Up Sheet

Date:

Children's room computers are for use by children age fourteen and younger. Computers may be used for 30 minutes. Please write your name below to use the computers.

Name	Time started	Time ended	Program Used

Readers' Advisory

Children's librarians provide readers' advisory services to the entire range of the public: toddler to teacher to grandparent. They booktalk titles individually to young people requesting suggestions. They suggest appropriate titles to child care workers and teachers who are developing units, and they make suggestions to parents and grandparents who are looking for books that are popular among and appropriate for specific ages of children.

While a background of reading widely in children's literature is useful for this service, professional resources are also helpful. Reading reviews, especially in *School Library Journal, Booklist,* and *Horn Book,* will give you a cursory knowledge about a book and its intended audience. Reading annual annotated lists, such as "Notable Books for Children," for several years back will add depth to that knowledge as well as provide titles you can recommend. Professional titles such as *Best Books for Children, What Do Children Read Next, Children's Catalog,* and *The Horn Book Guide* provide indexed listings with suggested grade levels, annotations, and subject listings.

When providing readers' advisory service to a specific child, ask for a title he really enjoyed or for a type of book he likes. It's much easier to connect a reader with a sequel, another mystery, or a sports story if you know his interests. His answer will also help you determine his reading ability, as grade level is not synonymous with ability level. While children will stretch their abilities to read books they are really interested in, for the most part, it is preferable to suggest titles in their ability range. If a book is too hard or too easy and they are not enthralled, young readers are not likely to complete it and may never return to it.

Inquire if the request is assignment-based. If it is, ask if there are teacher guidelines for the student's choice. Some teachers require students to read a minimum number of pages or a specific type of book, and you can save time and be more helpful if you know these requirements at the start.

Advising teachers can be either readers' advisory or reference. Refer the teacher who wants a good book to read aloud to third and fourth graders to *For Reading Out Loud* and *The New Read Aloud Handbook.* You could also suggest titles from your personal experience—Sid Fleischman's *The Whipping Boy,* Patricia MacLachlan's *Sarah Plain and Tall,* or Vedat Dalokay's *Sister Shako and Kolo the Goat,* for example, would all be appropriate. To both a preschool teacher and a fifth-grade teacher looking for materials on pre-Columbian America and Columbus, you could suggest *Best Books for Children* and back issues of *Book Links*. When helping teachers, it is very important to know grade level to provide an appropriate range. While, for example, scientific principles don't change, how they are explained for kindergartners and sixth graders does, and both approaches may be needed for a fourth grade class.

The indexes of *A to Zoo*, *Best Books for Children*, and *Children's Catalog*, and to a lesser extent *The Horn Book Guide*, are invaluable for finding a variety of titles on a wide range of subjects and ability levels. Whether you need picture books about being neat for preschoolers or non-fiction coverage of the problems of solid waste management for fifth graders, these books will help you find the materials.

Helping parents find books for their children is another readers' advisory function. If the child is with the parent, talk to her about what she likes and has read lately. A child who likes dog stories and recently read Rosemary Wells' *McDuff and the Baby* is probably not ready for Beverly Cleary's *Strider* or Fred Gibson's *Old Yeller*, but she could be able to handle *The Original Adventures of Hank the Cowdog*, by John Erickson. If the child is not present, elicit this type of information from her parent and make suggestions accordingly.

Asking the parent how the book will be used—for bedtime story reading, a book report assignment, or to address specific concerns, such as starting a new school, for example—will also help you make appropriate suggestions. Depending on the age of the child and how a book will be used, you should mention any aspects that might be problematic in particular books that you suggest. Charlotte dying at the end of *Charlotte's Web*, by E.B. White, and the wolf consuming the first and second pig in *The True Story of the Three Little Pigs* by A. Wolf as told to Jon Scieszka may be unwelcome developments. Advise parents to read books before sharing them with their children to avoid unwanted surprises.

Remember to treat all readers' advisory requests with respect. Do not allow your personal opinions about books or types of books to color your responses or service. For example, just because you don't like dog stories doesn't mean the child requesting one won't enjoy it. If you notice a child taking out a book you didn't enjoy, ask him (without letting him know your feelings about the book) to report back to you about how he liked it and what he liked about it.

Homework Support

Providing homework support service means assisting children in finding the information they need to complete their assignments. It does not mean doing their homework for them but rather directing them to the resources that hold the answers. Thus, you help a child find the exports of Brazil, but you don't explain a math problem (the first request is for information, while the second is a request for instruction).

Many libraries provide study centers for homework support. The study centers range from simple table space where a child can study away from home distractions to dedicated areas including tutors and computers with Internet homework help sites bookmarked. Regardless of how elaborate your library's study center is, a school supplies box would also be a welcome addition.

St. Louis Public Library maintains a tote box of school supplies at the reference desk in each children's area. Stocked with notebook paper, pencils, pens, tape, scissors, a stapler, protractor, and ruler, it is available so children can successfully complete assignments while they are at the library even if they forget some needed equipment. The boxes also free up the reference staff from interruptions to "borrow" something.

The philosophy behind providing homework support is grounded in the belief that going to school is a child's work. Just as a public library supports businesspeople's information search for their business, it should also support children in their school-related search for information. The single exception to providing homework support is when the teacher informs you that the assignment is a learning tool to reinforce library instruction the children have received.

The line between general reference service and homework support is very thin. Good homework support is good reference service, but several other children may need the same information at the same time each year. Because homework support tends to be cyclical, it is useful to maintain assignments files by grade, teacher, and school. If possible, photocopy the assignment sheet from the first student who comes in with a new assignment. Add the name of the teacher, class, school, and date to the photocopy, note successful search strategies and materials on the back, and put the sheet in the assignments file.

The reference interview for homework support is especially important because of the nature of children and homework. Children doing an assignment are less likely to know what they want than children researching a personal interest. Not only do they remember imperfectly, they sometimes assume that a single book or web site will have all the answers in terms that exactly match their assignment. It is important to question them carefully and explain that the concept of research is collecting information from a variety of sources. Talking and walking them through your search process is also helpful.

In an effort to provide better homework support, libraries over the years have used assignment alert forms and reference excuse slips. The assignment alert attempts to learn ahead of time about assignments and are filled out by teachers and sent to the library. They alert the library staff that a specific assignment has been made, what the students have been asked for, and when it is due. You can send blank assignment alert forms to the schools in the fall; you can also post them on your library's Web page with a link to the children's librarian. A sample assignment alert form appears on page 20. The reference excuse forms verify to the teacher that the library was not able to help a particular student with the assignment.

Reference excuse slips are filled out by the librarian and sent back to the school. They alert the teacher that a specific student came to the library on a specific day, the student requested information about a specific topic, and the library was unable to fill the request. The reference excuse slip usually has options you can check off, such as material requested is too new or too old, no books are available about it, all available material in circulation, and so on. The slip includes a request for the teacher to contact the library before making the assignment again so that you can be prepared for it in the future. A sample reference excuse form appears on page 21.

Sample Assignment Alert Form

Library Name:_____ Branch Name: _____
_____ Branch Phone: _____
_____ Branch Fax:_____

Teachers! Help us help your students. Please send us information about upcoming school assignments using the form below. Deliver, mail, or fax it to us at least one week prior to the assignment. You may also complete this form on our web site:

Dates of Assignment: _____ to _____

Teacher:_____ Phone: _____
Fax:_____ e-mail: _____
(Please indicate the most convenient way for us to reach you if we have a question)

School: _____ Grade:_____ Number of students:

1. Description of Assignment

    What kind of information are students expected to find?

    What are the details of the assignment?

2. Indicate each type of source required for completion of assignment:

    ___ Any source may be used   ___ Books

    ___ Reference materials   ___ Magazines

    ___ Newspapers   ___ Internet

    ___ Library databases

3. Often the underlying purpose of assignments is to teach students how to use the library. How much assistance do you want us to provide?

    Yes/No

    Demonstrate the use of library catalog?

    Demonstrate use of materials?

    Suggest appropriate titles?

    Provide information over the phone?

    Let student find on their own?

4. Please list books, magazines, reference materials, internet sites or other resources that you recommend for this assignment.

Sample Reference Excuse Slip

Name of Library:_____

Name of Branch: _____

Teacher's name: _____ Date: _____

(Student name)_____
came to the library today. We regret that we were unable to fill
the request for

_____

Reasons:

_____ All circulating material is in use because of the large
        student demand for material on this subject.

_____ Reference material in this area is limited.

_____ A reasonable amount of research failed to turn up the
        desired information.

A request was left by the student for materials when they become
available ____yes ____no.

Could we work together on the availability of material for your
future class assignments? Please contact me at _____ or
place your assignment on the Assignment Alert form on our web site

_____

_____
                    Librarian

3

Storytime and Storytelling

Storytime

One of the most familiar activities offered in virtually every library is the storytime. Library storytimes are literacy-building activities. Since the promotion and support of literacy is integral to everything a children's librarian does, providing storytimes is an important activity. Planning and implementing a storytime can also be one of the most intimidating things that a new librarian has to do. The encouraging thing you should remember about doing storytime is that children will enjoy sharing books and activities with you.

It is important to present a well-planned program. While seasoned children's librarians may improvise for storytime, a program with some structure to it, typically working with a theme and a routine, generally is more successful.

Scheduling

Storytime scheduling is an art. Schedule a series of six, eight, or ten weeks, with a couple of weeks break between series. With careful planning, this schedule allows breaks for the holidays, the end of May, and the end of August and early September, when attendance typically drops off. This schedule gives staff a break and it also allows you to do a "Start Up of

Storytime" promotion. As your populations grow or shrink, you will need to reassess the number and types of storytimes scheduled.

Themes

Your library may already have its storytime themes planned and a routine developed. In this case, all you should need to do is first practice the stories and then go with the theme. To become more comfortable with an already planned program, you might want to add something personal to it—an old camp song you know, a poem, or a show-and-tell item that goes along with the stories—to help make your presentation uniquely yours.

If you are not working with a preselected theme, you may want to begin by choosing a theme. Themes can be general (such as the letter e, celebrations, or great pictures), or specific (for example, alligators and crocodiles, around the farm, or trains). Once you have selected a theme, you can start collecting the component parts of the storytime—picture books, fingerplays, poems, flannel board stories, short videos, songs, activities, and so on.

Plan four to six weeks' worth of themes at a time. This planning will save you time in searching for the parts—what won't work for one week's theme might work for another. If you will be presenting multiple storytimes for different age groups, try using the same theme so that you can reuse material that is appropriate.

Check to see if files of past storytime programs are available. They could lead you to some great books in the collection and shortcut the planning process for you. You may be able to freshen up older storytimes with new books or videos.

Many books provide complete storytime sessions, such as Jeri Kladder's *Story Hour: 55 Preschool Programs for Public Libraries*, Judy Nichols's *Storytimes for Two-Year-Olds*, and Rob Reid's *Family Storytime*. These books have tried-and-true suggestions of books and activities. Studying them is also useful just to see what books and activities have been put together successfully, what routine is followed, and the proportion of book reading to other activities. Books are also available that index the component parts, such as *A to Zoo* and *Move Over, Mother Goose!*

Keep a file of storytime programs because, unlike the population served by the adult services department, your audience will turn completely over in four years and then you can use these programs again. A good program can be used more frequently: holiday storytimes are repeated annually and others every two to three years. The really popular programs can be presented again as "Favorite Storytimes."

One library has a voting process like the Oscars to determine the annual favorites; it then repeats the three top vote-getters as special programs during the summer when regular storytime is in hiatus.

Selecting and Preparing Storytime Material

When selecting books for storytime, use an index like *A to Zoo* to help you identify titles. Gather more material than you can imagine using, and take time to go through all the books in one sitting. Decide which books you want to read, which you could booktalk, and which are not appropriate for your group. Keep track of books that might work for another theme. Place holds on all possible material and then select the ones you want.

When you select books to read aloud, look for large clear pictures and a simple, not too wordy text with pleasing language. Fairly large type is helpful if you haven't memorized the story. No matter how delightful, seek-and-find books are not appropriate for storytime.

If a book is too long to read in its entirety, you can paraphrase it or just talk about the pictures. Relevant nonfiction often fits in this category. The longer books can be made available in a book browse.

Choose books in good condition. Worn-out books with scribbling in them give the wrong impression. If a favorite starts showing wear, order a replacement; if it is a real favorite, order two so that one can circulate and the other copy can be kept in your storytime collection.

Prioritize the stories with the longest or most relevant one first. Read the books over several times before presenting them. Read them at least once aloud. Remember to practice holding the book so the children can see the pictures.

Always have a couple of back up stories ready even if they barely relate to the theme. There will be times that you will need them.

Gather and practice your fingerplays and songs. Some fingerplay sources give the words only, so you may have to think up appropriate motions. You may also need to adapt fingerplays and songs; if the children are seated on the floor, for example, you probably don't want to use a song that has the children standing up and sitting back down in quick succession. Plan the more active fingerplays and songs for the end of the session.

Look for poetry, puppets, and realia to work into your program. Children's poetry is wonderful to drop in between books or other activities. The rhythm, rhyme, and vocabulary of poems add a great deal to children's language development and understanding, and many of them are just plain fun.

A puppet doesn't have to say much to add something. Use one to introduce a book. For example, I have a fly finger puppet that I buzz around before reading *Old Black Fly* to two- and three-year-olds (I also slap the "swat" page for effect). You can use a puppet to lead the singing, as the birthday puppet, or as a booktalk puppet. Caroline Bauer's *New Handbook for Storytellers* and *Leading Children to Books through Puppets* give lots of workable, do-able ideas.

Realia (Latin for real) is a term used to describe "real" items, such as a train whistle, engineer's hat, or lantern (all realia that you might use for a program on trains). You can use realia anytime during the storytime as a discussion starter or story lead-in. Realia are fun but not essential to each storytime; for example, if you are doing a fishy storytime and you already have a fish print picture, bring it out to show and share, but don't buy one. Mention to coworkers or put a wishlist on the bulletin board of things you could use, such as a hank of fleece, carding pads, and some thread or yarn to use with *Charlie Needs a Cloak*.

Plan for discussion about the stories' action during the program. Draw attention to realia, pictures, and other items around the children's area that relate to the story or the theme. This relation helps children make connections, and it models to parents and caregivers how to expand the learning process. If you have the capability, prepare a handout for the parents with the words to the fingerplays and songs.

Storytime Area and Help

Give some consideration to the setup of the storytime area. Some libraries have separate storytime rooms, while others make do with moving some tables out of the way for floor space. Your available area will impact the kind of storytimes you present and what kind of guidelines you develop.

Have the children sit with their backs to the entrance doorway and windows, so that they will be less distracted and you will be able to hold their attention more easily. You can have the children sit on the floor and put books, flannel board, and other materials on tables on either side of your chair. Stack all the materials in the order they will be used. A bookcart also works well to hold these items.

Set up only a few chairs at the back and edges for adults, and announce, "Chairs are for people over sixteen." Some libraries don't set up any chairs but instead have everyone sit on the floor, with taller participants at the edges.

If you are having crafts, set up worktables away from the story area if possible. Cover the tables with inexpensive plastic tablecloths to protect them from gluing and coloring. Keep crayons in little baskets or plastic tubs.

If the group is large (and even if it isn't), an assistant can help with name tags and can keep control at the back of the room. The assistant can control the lights, count the participants, and keep order, allowing you to present the storytime.

Routines

A storytime routine is important. It provides a comfortable structure for the children and helps pace the program.

An appropriate length of time for the storytime program is critical. For an audience younger than thirty months, about twenty minutes start to finish is enough. Three- to five-year-olds can usually handle thirty minutes. Children under seven years old are unlikely to be able to concentrate for programs over forty-five minutes long. Groups of mixed ages of children with their parents can usually pay attention longer than narrower age groups without parents.

If you are expected to prepare a longer program, extend the session with open-ended activities. Display picture books that tie into the day's theme (a good use of those back-up books you selected) for browsing, or offer simple make-and-take craft activities (make a stick puppet by adding features to a cut-out shape and taping it to a plastic straw or craft stick). Children can color in groups on a theme-related coloring sheet while you booktalk to parents and care givers about related books—this activity lets you extend the storytime without requiring the children simply to sit quietly.

A typical routine might include:

Greeting and making name tags

Opening activity

First book reading

Second book

Fingerplay, song, or activity

Third book

Story in a different format

Fingerplay, song, or activity

Closing activity, book browse

NAME TAGS

Name tags can help you learn and use the children's names so that you can encourage them by name to join in or respond. If you preregister children for storytime, you can make their name tags in advance. Name tags relating to the theme are nice. Diecut shapes come in very handy as name tags, although construction paper squares, decorated with a sticker or rubber stamp, work fine too.

Ask the parents or caregivers to write the child's first name on the name tag and to tape it to the child's shirt. You might want to use name tags over and over. If so, laminating will help their longevity, as will putting them on ribbon or yarn necklaces for the children to wear instead of taping them on. Collect them at the end of the program.

For safety reasons and guarding the children's privacy, nametags should be kept out of view when not in use. Remind parents and caregivers to remove the nametags before they leave the program area.

OPENING ACTIVITIES

The opening activity can take a variety of formats. I do the fingerplay "Open, Shut Them," as it leaves the children with their hands folded in their laps. You can sing a welcome song, do a one- or two-item show and tell, use a storytime puppet to greet the children, or just talk with the children about the day's theme as they look at the books and items displayed on a table. Before starting a storytime with singing, warm up your voice a little.

READINGS AND FINGERPLAYS

The first book you'll read is usually the longest or most relevant to your theme. Point out things in the pictures as appropriate. For example, when you read the James Marshall illustrated version of *The Night before Christmas,* you can point out the chickens, St. Nick's cowboy boots, and his refrigerator raiding. Take a poll, asking the children by show of hands if they think Santa is after the lima beans or the chocolate cream pie. After you read it, talk about it a bit and then move to the second book.

After you read the second book, do a fingerplay or sing a song with the children. If the fingerplay is new, it helps to walk the children through it line by line before putting it all together. You may need to repeat a finger-play or song two to three times if it is new or popular. Eager requests to "do it again" can be indulged.

If you play a musical instrument like a guitar, ukulele, autoharp, or keyboard, consider working it into the song. Some people incorporate books with electronic music chips into the song. You can sing along with children's song tapes, too; however, the children tend to sing faster or slower or not at all, and trying to start and stop at the right place can make using the song tapes difficult. (Recorded opening music and closing music are the exception.)

Read a third book, and then do a story in a different format—traditional storytelling, flannel board, or big book. This piece can be another version of a story already read or a complimentary one. Do not overlook using the flannel board story format because you think it old-fashioned. Today's high-tech children are not immune to the magic of a story or poem unfolding before their eyes.

Flannel Boards

Flannel boards can be purchased, or you can staple or glue felt to a rectangle of heavy-duty cardboard, half-inch foam core, or a piece of acoustic ceiling tile. Flannel board pieces are easily made with patterns—see the bibliography for sources, or copy them from clip art books and adjust the size with a photocopier. Use medium- to heavy-weight fabric interfacing (not the fusible type), a fine-line permanent black marker, crayons (I recommend a big box with lots of colors), and sharp scissors. Trace the pattern onto the fabric with the fine-line marker, color it before you cut it, and then cut shape out. Attach a copy of the text or poem that you will be reading to the back of the flannel board or hold it in your lap for presentation.

After you present a story in another format, present another fingerplay or song, perhaps repeating the first one or singing new verses.

OTHER ACTIVITIES

You can follow your final reading with a large motor activity—acting out a portion of a story or an activity rhyme, for example. This activity allows the children to "get their wiggles out." Alternatively, you might show a video if appropriate and available; use only videos to which your library owns public performance rights.

If you want to include a craft program, consider how extensive it should be. If you are working with very young children, for example, their abilities are quite limited. Be careful that the craft activity doesn't overshadow the book experience. If you do have crafts, consider making them project oriented. The children can work on something over a period of weeks for an end result, such as making a torn paper collage cover for the alphabet color sheets that they have been taking home each week, or making pompons and hats for a Fourth of July parade through a local nursing home.

CLOSING ACTIVITY

Your closing activity could include a goodbye song, a verbal wrap-up about the books shared, announcing next week's theme, having the children put their name tags in a special place, or booktalking displayed books.

Storytime Outline Record

Create an outline that gives the books' titles and authors and keep it handy during the storytime. If there is a special announcement (such as a child's birthday or information about an up coming program) you want to make, write it on the outline as a memory aid. At the end of the program you can date the outline, note the attendance, staple a sample name tag to it or note which die-cut shape was used, attach any handout materials, and add any pertinent comments regarding how the materials went over or their condition. The outline then becomes your record of the program.

Storytelling

Storytelling, as opposed to story reading to a library audience, appears more daunting than it actually is. Newer children's librarians may believe they could never tell stories, especially if they have heard professional storytellers in concert. Remember than an audience of four- and five-year-olds will be happy hearing you tell "The Three Billy Goats Gruff" with a grouchy troll and a lot of trip-trapping over the bridge.

Everyone is a storyteller. When you told the teacher that your dog ate your homework, you were telling a story. Just because it didn't start with "Once upon a time" doesn't mean it wasn't a story.

In learning a story you plan to present as a storyteller, choose one you already know and like. Select a story you are already familiar with, and the learning process will go faster. A classic folktale like "The Three Bears," "The Three Little Pigs," or "The Little Red Hen" is a good choice. Choose only stories you personally like. Stories you don't like will take much longer to learn and are never as effective to tell.

Whenever you are reading stories, make a file of those you think would be good told. Photocopy these stories and note the author, title, and page numbers within the book in which the story appears. This file can save you hours of time searching for just the right story in the future.

Choose stories that are appropriate for your audience—don't talk down or over their heads. Fifth- and sixth-graders may relish hearing you tell a story from Patricia McKissack's *The Dark Thirty*, but this collection is not right for five- and six-year-olds.

Be sure you know the definitions of all the words in the story. Four-year-olds may not know that porridge is like oatmeal or that a cauldron is a big cooking pot. You can share them with your audience as long as you do so unobtrusively.

Read several versions of the story you have selected. Read through the version you like best several times more, at least once aloud. If you are not thoroughly familiar with the plot line, take notes of the main points and action. Think out the personalities of the characters. Is Big Billy Goat Gruff a bully or businesslike? Is the Middle-sized Billy Goat a loud girl or a shy one? Does the troll remind you of cousin Bobby?

You don't need to memorize a story, but you should memorize the phrases or descriptions that are crucial to the flavor and meaning of the story. What would "The Three Little Pigs" be without "Little Pig, Little Pig, let me in!" and "Not by the hair of my chinny chin chin."

Practice telling the story aloud or to yourself to help set the pace of the story, the intonations, and the dynamics. If you tell it too fast or too slowly, too softly or with a high pitched voice, you will not create the mood you want.

Practice in front of a mirror to watch your body language. As you tell stories more often, you may want to add small gestures or other body movement to help you visually define story characters.

Watch videos of professional storytellers to pick up storytelling pointers. When you tell the story to an audience, work on making eye contact with the children. This personalizes the experience for them and helps deter misbehavior.

Use props sparingly and only if appropriate—the storyteller creates with words, not with hats, stuffed monkeys, plastic kettles, or large spoons.

Consider the storytelling setting. A noisy, brightly lit area will make your story less effective than a quiet area with subdued lighting.

Consider branching out with participation stories. Having your audience join in increases the fun.

Do include storytelling as part of story programs. It increases the wonder of words for children.

4

Variety Programming for Children

Storytime and storytelling may be the most common and traditional type of library programming for children, but many libraries offer other kinds of programs and summer reading programs as well. Children's library programming can include (but is not limited to) craft and film programs, book discussion groups, "discovery times," speakers, puppet shows, musicians, and special events. A sample variety program appears at the end of this chapter.

Starting Variety Programming

If your library already offers variety programming, you can continue what has already been established. Consult the existing planning, promotional, and budgeting timetables and schedules to learn when you will need to start planning the next season's events, and mark those deadlines on your calendar.

Instituting variety programming where none has been in place requires careful consideration, funds, time, and administrative support. All library programs, especially those for children, should connect in some way with the books and materials they will find in the library. As you consider offering variety programming, ask yourself these types of questions:

Does additional programming fit into your library's goals and chosen roles?

Is there a written or unwritten cost/benefit ratio in regards to programs at your library?

Do you have sufficient staff support and interest to carry it off well?

Do you have enough long-term planning and preparation time?

Who is your audience—families, preschoolers, or elementary age children?

Will you offer one type of variety programming or more? How frequently—once a week, a month, or a season?

Is your space conducive to variety programming—have you considered floor and ceiling space, electrical outlets, lighting, sound system, and occupancy limits?

If you bring in an outside performer and the response is overwhelming, do you have contingency plans?

What about programs offered freely by business persons in return for publicity and contacts, such as children's music schools or local children's book authors?

What evaluative criteria will be used to consider a program a success or failure?

If your library offers variety programming but attendance is falling off, you may want to rethink what you are doing and for whom. Demographics and public needs change over time. Now that videos and VCRs are ubiquitous, library movie programs are no longer the draw they once were. Offering two programs may not be better than one but instead just splits the available audience.

Planning Variety Programming

Many professional resources, including Caroline Bauer's *New Handbook for Storytellers*, offer programming ideas. State-created reading program manuals from past years are another useful resource. If you are at a loss for ideas, consider repeating successful programs from previous years as "Golden Oldies." Unlike most adults, children like repetition, and the population of children turns over much more quickly, too.

Keep good records (and copies of all relevant parts) of programs—resources, planning time involved, patterns, contacts, contracts, publicity, and evaluations. Good files can save hours of time, prevent mistakes, and make next year's planning easier. Access to good files will also make your job easier.

Keep a presenter file in conjunction with your programming records. The presenter file can be part of a larger community resource file, or you can organize it as a department-specific file. This file should contain the names, phone numbers, and addresses both for local individual performers (storytellers, clowns, magicians, musicians, puppeteers, parent educators, and ventriloquists) and for contact people or positions in the public sector that can act as resources (fire, police, and parks departments, for example).

If the presenter file is publicly available, you may want to include phone numbers of some references and some indication as to the fees charged by different presenters. You can indicate fee levels with one, two, or three dollar signs, as some travel guides do.

Hiring Professional Program Presenters

Sometimes libraries that offer variety programming have the budget to hire professional storytellers, clowns, magicians, and so on, or to pay an author to speak. These kinds of programs need to meet the before-mentioned criteria for variety programming, but they also have some additional requirements.

Plan ahead. You will have greater success at getting the speaker or performer you want if you make contact six to eight months (or more) in advance.

Do some preliminary work prior to contacting a speaker or performer. Ask other librarians if they have ever heard the speaker or seen the performer and what did they think. See if there's a web site with information on the person. Contact an author or illustrator's publisher or check the presenter's web site to find out if he or she visits libraries, the contact information, and a ballpark speaking fee. Some authors would rather write than speak, or don't do well with children, and it is better to know this before you spend time trying to contact them.

Be clear about what you offer to and expect from the presenter. Besides how much money you have available for the program, be sure to have room dimensions, sound equipment availability, expected audience size, lodging arrangements, and transportation options handy when you make contact, as well as a brief summary of the kind of program you want. Puppeteers can't bring a marionette show if your room has only ten-foot ceilings, and that very nice storyteller may not want to spend the night in your guest room because she is allergic to cats.

Once you have made contact and settled on dates and fees (being very clear on who pays for what and when), you will want to develop a contract for services that spells out the parameters of the performance. This contract, which both of you must sign, can save you many headaches. You should add the checklist of information in the accompanying box to the contract as another safeguard against problems.

Ask the presenter for publicity materials that may help you liven up the program promotion. Publicity pictures are especially nice and will set the program off from other library events, as will a special sketch or performer-supplied poster.

Does the performer plan to distribute a business card or brochure? Clarify if the presenter expects to sell tapes, books, or other materials either before or after the performance and who will be responsible for taking orders, making change, returning unsold inventory, and so on.

Find out if the performer needs to be met at the airport, a hotel, or the library door. Do you need to provide help for moving equipment into the library? How much help will be needed? How much time is needed to set up? Is the library expected to provide any special equipment, such as a ladder, computer, surge protector, or power strip? What size of table, type of chair, or brand of bottled water is requested? Will the presenter need a place to change clothes or apply makeup?

Are the audience size guidelines hard and fast, or can a few more people be slipped in? How many more?

Checklist of Information to Provide to Professional Program Presenters

___ full name of the sponsoring institution

___ the name of the facility where the program will take place, if different than above

___ the facility's complete address, telephone number, fax number, and email address

___ the name of the individual responsible for the booking

___ the name of the individual responsible for the on-site hosting or supervision of the event

___ contract signed and returned

___ the method and time of payment (typically right after the performance)

___ the precise nature of your programming expectations

___ the target audience and the number of attendees expected

___ information about any special library goals or seasonal themes
that should be worked into the presentation

___ for an out-of-town speaker, an informal descriptive profile of the
community

Sometimes a performer who is too expensive for you to bring in on your own is willing to do several shows for several different groups. The groups can then divide the transportation and lodging costs among themselves. Find out if the presenter is agreeable to this option, but be sure that who pays for what is clearly spelled out between the cooperating agencies.

When the show is over, be sure that the performer has help breaking down the equipment, packing it up, and hauling it out. Be sure that payment is made as agreed upon. It's nice to send copies of any local media coverage the program may generate and to share any thank-you notes you get, in a follow-up letter.

For more in-depth information about inviting an author or illustrator, consult *Inviting Children's Authors and Illustrators: A How-to-Do-It Manual for School and Public Librarians,* by Kathy East (Neal-Schuman, 1995).

Sample Variety Program:
A Live Pet Show

The steps involved in planning and implementing a successful program are essentially the same. The following example exemplifies these steps.

All library programs for children are intended to increase the visibility of the library and its resources. A live pet show is an easy and inexpensive variety program which does just that while the young customers and staff all have fun, too. This program requires only timely planning, some award ribbons, water containers, a loud voice or portable microphone, a staff assistant, and a grassy area by the library. The program described here was offered for children of all ages with their families, with up to sixty partici-pants and audience members.

Planning the Pet Show

Because the animals in a pet show need to be outside, plan a time when the weather is clement, usually during the summer. A grassy area under a large tree or on the north side of the building works well in the summer. If it's been dry, plan to water the area several times in the days before the show.

Four to five weeks before the pet show, put up posters announcing it. The posters and any handout materials should make clear that all pets must come on leashes or in cages and that their owners must be in control of them at all time. If there are any types of pets you would rather not have (snakes, for instance) include that information on the posters and flyers, using phrasing such as "furry, feathered, or finny pets only."

Send a press release to the local paper and follow up with an invitation to have a reporter/photographer cover the event. Pet show participants are very photogenic, and newspaper photographs are a good way to generate positive publicity about the library.

Prepare a form or sign-up sheet. Participants should include their names, type of pet, and phone number.

If you know of someone in the community who has an award-winning show pet, invite the pet owner to share the animal for a few minutes with the children. Also ask for any professional pictures and ribbons won by the pet that you can display. One year a grandfatherly gentleman with a National Champion Boston Terrier attended one of the pet shows I was doing, and together they quite stole the show.

Prepare enough rosette ribbons for everyone signed up, plus twelve to eighteen extra. Make them all the same color. Floral ribbon works well for this. Hang each ribbon on a yarn cord and add a white tag for noting the pet's award.

One or two days before, call and remind those who signed up. Remind them again that all pets must be on leashes or in cages.

The Day of the Show

Set up a few chairs for adults in the back of the pet show area. Leave the center area empty for the children and their pets. Set out a small table or book cart at the front to hold the ribbons, a marker, and a book or two for sharing if appropriate. Set up a sound system, if available, and tape down any cords that might trip someone.

Fill several containers with water for the pets and set them out of the way.

As families and pets gather, announce that chairs are for those over sixteen and that children and their pets are welcome to sit on the grass. Point out where the water is.

Start the program by welcoming the participants and presenting how the pet show will be conducted. Explain that all pets are winners, so all pets will receive a ribbon. Clarify that the pets will be shown in groups by species. Ask by show of hands how many brought dogs, cats, rodents, fish, and other animals.

It's best to take the largest group first—usually dogs. Ask the children in the first group to come up front with their pets, four to six at a time. Have them line up facing the audience.

Walk down the line and stop at each child. Ask the child's name and the pet's name. Make some positive comment about the pet and decide what aspect is most noteworthy—for example, is it the fluffiest, does it have the most spots, is it well trained, does it have the longest tongue? Have your assistant write that characteristic on a rosette ribbon tag. Give the ribbon to the child, and move on to the next pet. (If more than one child accompanies an individual pet, make multiple ribbons for that pet so each child receives one). Have the group go back to their seats.

After the dogs, you can tell the story "Why Dogs Chase Cats" from *The Knee High Man and Other Tales.* Pet jokes, a pet trick demonstration, or some other pet story or book would fit in here too.

Work your way through the cats and the rest of the pets.

Be ready for the special case. A four-year-old child might bring pictures of his two cats, which would still be deserving of a ribbon.

Do a "last call" for any late arriving pets and tell folks where pet and animal care books may be found in the collection.

If there are any exotic or champion pets, you can introduce the pet and its owner as the program's grande finale. Allow the owner to show the fine points of the animal.

Complete the show by thanking everyone for sharing their award-winning animals.

Summer Reading Programs

5

Coordinating a library's summer reading program takes long-range planning, attention to detail, and stamina. Only the regular storytime program consumes more time and attention.

Planning the Program

Learn your library's philosophy on a summer reading program. Is it intended to develop lifelong learners or encourage reading for pleasure? Is it expected to boost circulation or help children maintain reading skills? While most likely the program is a combination of these, understanding why your library promotes the program will help you in producing it and in knowing what areas to emphasize.

Find out where in the total library budget the summer reading program falls to help you plan. For instance, a summer reading program budgeted as a public relations/library promotion program is funded differently and more generously than items in the programming budget, but it also comes with the responsibility to do more promotion.

If your library lacks funds for a summer reading program, consider applying for the ALSC/Book Wholesalers Summer Reading Program Grant. Available to members of ALA and ALSC, this grant of $3000 underwrites an innovative public library theme-based summer reading program that includes all children birth through fourteen. It especially encourages innovative proposals involving children with physical or mental disabilities. Applications are due the first of December for the next summer.

As with other programming, your library may have already developed a summer reading program and methodology that you can use. Using an existing program format means that many time-consuming parts or policy level decisions have already been developed or decided. Check timelines and note deadlines on your calendar. A good summer program is the result of year-round planning and preparation. Does storytime continue throughout the summer? Do you schedule school visits to promote the program in May?

If you are asked to start a summer reading program, discuss with your administrator the program's goals and audience. The goal of the summer reading program the author coordinates is promoting the library and encouraging a lifelong love of reading. The program counts books read, includes children from birth through the eighth grade, runs the entire summer (from June 1 to the last Saturday in August), invites childcare providers to read library books to the children in their care and provides incentives for all the listening children, offers contracts to special reading students that allow them to set their own reading goals, and uses paperback books as incentives. The books are paid for by the library. The program is very successful, and it makes summers very busy.

Summer Reading Program Goals and Audience Consideration

Is the program for only K-6 children, or should it include preschoolers and teens?

Will only high-volume readers be recognized or will participants be allowed to set their own goals and recognition be more general?

Will you count the number of books read, or will you count total time spent reading?

Are the joys of reading and accomplishment and a certificate adequate incentive, or do you need to have additional prizes?

Will all who meet the program's goals be recognized equally?

How long should the program run?

Can children in childcare participate as a group?

Program Components

Study past programs to determine the components involved in your program. Consider whether you need to schedule extra programs, including selecting and hiring presenters, booking meeting rooms, and determining the budget. Is the reading log unique to each year, or is a generic form used? What other printing is needed and in what quantities? What incentives will be used and have they been lined up? Will you need to canvas local businesses for gift certificates and coupons? Books that correspond to the program's theme or that are recommended reading might need to be added to the collection. Determine who orders these book and when they should be ordered.

Here again professional books are available for guidance. Carole Fiore's *Running Summer Library Programs* is written from her broad experience as Florida State Children's Consultant and managing Florida's statewide program. She gives step-by-step directions on planning a program and provides information on how to be inclusive with special populations of children. Past state reading program manuals are also valuable guides to how to do these programs.

Programming materials may need to be ordered from the state library or supplier very early on. Some states and suppliers cut overruns very close to keep down costs. As a result, those T-shirts or posters may not be available after the deadline, which can be as early as February!

Keep good records of participants; this information will help you in many ways. Use a simple registration card with places to indicate the child's name, address, grade and school, and completions. Transfer the registration information to an electronic database for recordkeeping.

Sample Reading Program Registration Card

SUMMER READING PROGRAM _____
                                    (year)

NAME: _____

ADDRESS: _____

PHONE: _____   AGE: _____

SCHOOL: _____   GRADE: _____

Lists Completed: 1 2 3 4 5 6 7 8 9

Sort the registrations (either on cards or in the electronic database) by school to show where you need to promote the program more next year. Sort them by grade to learn who is most attracted to your program. You can compare the total number of registrations to the total number of eligible children to get the percentage of the population that your program served.

Knowing this percentage can help you plan for measurable outcomes, such as increasing participation from the west part of town by 5 percent. This information is also helpful if you solicit incentives. You can tell local merchants, "Our records show that 25 percent of children who participate in the reading program live in your service area. Wouldn't you like to increase your donation of coupons so that all those children can earn one?"

Jill Locke, in her unpublished doctoral thesis, determined that average participation in reading programs is 3 to 4 percent of eligible children. If your program attracts 7 percent, you're doing well. Remember, summer reading program participation can be a building process.

Administering the Program

Prior to the actual start of the program, go over the procedures and guidelines with all staff, including pages and volunteers.

I stress to my staff that one of the goals of our program is to create readers for pleasure and the quickest way I can think of to squelch a child's pleasure in reading is to tell her the book she's selected is too easy. Staff members should never belittle a child's choice of reading material as too easy. If you feel a child is capable of more challenging books, you can suggest titles that you feel are appropriate and leave it at that.

Make it clear to the staff that the summer reading program operates on the honor system. The staff should accept without question the children's reports of their reading accomplishments. Ideally, once the reading program starts, all there is left to do is welcome the children to the library and enjoy it.

Day-to-Day Running the Program

Handling the day-to-day mechanics of a summer reading program depends on the amount of control you want to have over it, the amount of space available, and the amount of staff time available.

You will need to decide if you want ongoing registration, where a child may sign up at any time during the program, or if you will limit sign-up time to the first week or two. You should also decide in advance if attendance at library programs counts for the summer reading program and how to measure it—does attending three programs count as three books read or forty-five minutes spent reading?

If you have enough space and staff time, try to set up a program registration desk (decorated if possible), away from the circulation or reference desk. Direct the children to this desk to sign up for the program, receive program materials, and have the program explained to them. Try to have a staff member fill out the registration card—it's more likely to be legible.

Take reasonable care with the registration cards, as they do have personal information on them about your participants. You can mark the tops with different colors by grade, school, or age to be able to tell at a glance if you have more K-2 readers or more participants from Southside Elementary.

Children or their parents can keep charge of their own reading logs by writing in titles or the minutes spent reading as they are completed. When a child returns a completed log, the staff member at the reading program desk should congratulate the child, rubber stamp or date the completed log and return it to the child, and mark the child's registration card with the completion. Then give the successful reader a reading certificate.

While I personally think giving the successful readers their certificates when they turn in their first completed logs will reinforce their accomplishment, many libraries hold end-of-program parties or celebrations and award the certificates and "prizes" then. If you are offering an escalating scale of incentives or planning a series of prize drawings, some sort of end-of-program event will be necessary. Attendance at these events shouldn't be mandatory for children to receive incentives they have earned or prizes they have won. At the start of the program, think of your arrangements for mailing or having children pick up their incentives and prizes so you can pass along the pertinent information to the children.

Updates to the media throughout the summer can keep interest high in the community. It is usually easy to get news coverage in August. Consider sending little filler articles, like "Library enrolls 20 percent more children in Summer Reading Program" to area papers along with photo opportunity program information. One program I did early in my career received national wire service coverage. We held a worm race at a particularly slow news time, and the local paper was eager for copy.

During the summer, update your administrator and library board on the progress of the program. I make a point to give current totals to my director right before the library board meets. Document the program for board members with display boards with photographs of reading program events placed on easels in the board room before the meetings. Board members can easily see the program in action, which has translated into continued high board support for the program.

At the end of the program, "debrief" the staff who participated in it. Be open to suggestions of ways to streamline or simplify the program but be ready to justify why some things have to continue being done in a certain way. Ask the staff which was their favorite event/program and their least favorite one, and why. Ask for suggestions for future programs, events, and presenters.

Program Evaluation and Follow-up

Be sure and evaluate the completed program for your files, your supervisor, and the library board. If expected goals were not met or were greatly exceeded, offer reasons why you believe you got the outcomes you did. One year, for example, flooding made several branch libraries inaccessible for two weeks during the reading program, leading to a negative effect on participation. Another year saw an enormous areawide media push on the value of summer reading, and we experienced unexpected double-digit growth in participation.

Detail for the board the amounts of materials and time that went into the program. I prepare a "Summer Reading Program at a Glance" sheet that lists statistics about the program, such as events presented and children attending each. This sheet graphically shows the board members what is involved and has a very positive impact on their support.

If you used a state-provided reading program, complete the evaluation form and send it in by the deadline. The state program needs those figures to justify the program to its funding agency. Any photographs and newspaper clippings you can send along to the state program will also be greatly appreciated as they help document the program's success.

Collection
Development

6

Children's librarians have other responsibilities besides front-line reference and programming. These other responsibilities include collection development, displays, preparing bibliographies, presenting booktalks, providing library instruction and library tours, doing outreach, and doing publicity. Many of these duties overlap the front-line ones; for example, library instruction is part of reference, and programming uses publicity and displays, but they can be separate responsibilities also.

Materials for a children's department are selected specifically for different ages, interests, and developmental levels. Books, magazines, electronic resources, and possibly audiovisual materials should be made available that give children immediate reading pleasure; satisfy their curiosity and desire for information on all subjects; and encourage a love of reading through this satisfaction and enjoyment as well as a feeling of security in the knowledge that there are sources to which they can go for information and pleasure.

When approaching collection development, first reread your library's selection policy and mission statement. Take special note of what the policy says in regard to children as library users and to materials for them. Material selection policies can be helpful in guiding your selection decisions and can support you in case of a complaint. Since the selection policy is approved by the library's administrative board, any purchased materials that fit within the context of the policy have the tacit approval of the administration and the board, hence giving the librarian the backing of her administration.

Letting conscientious collection development slide in favor of simply purchasing well-reviewed new books as they come out will cause problems in the future. A children's collection, like all quality collections, takes constant maintenance on five fronts: ongoing evaluation, the core collection, new materials, nonprint media, and replacements.

Ongoing Evaluation

Evaluating a children's collection follows the same procedure as evaluating an adult collection, with the added caveat of age appropriateness. When evaluating the collection, ask yourself regarding each book:

1. Is its topic of current interest? Does it have historical or regional value or interest?
2. Has its information been superseded by new materials? Is a revised edition with substantial changes now available?
3. Is its appearance, content, or illustration outdated?
4. Is it accurate?
5. How frequently has it circulated?
6. What is its condition? Is it tattered, smelly, or warped?
7. Are there more multiple copies than needed?
8. Is it unique to the collection as to information or viewpoint?
9. Does it appeal to a special group in the community—for example, is the author or setting local?
10. Can you afford to replace it?

Some libraries have an arbitrary circulation cut-off of two or three years (often set because of limited space)—a book that has not circulated within that time will be withdrawn from the collection. Be sure and look over any books pulled for noncirculation to make sure important core materials are not inadvertently withdrawn. For example, a book about a particular American state may not have circulated in the last three years but should be retained.

Questions on a book's continuing accuracy, whether later editions have been published, and so forth can be answered by evaluating the collection against the subject area in *Children's Catalog*. As you identify titles in the collection that are listed in *Children's Catalog,* make a note in the corner of the book's flyleaf (i.e., "CC99" for *Children's Catalog 1999)* and make a checkmark in *Children's Catalog* at the entry. Follow this procedure as you add new books to the collection. This practice is especially helpful in building a core collection, because a glance through the *Children's Catalog* will show what is owned. It also saves time in ordering replacements.

Once you have evaluated a book, you must decide what the next step is. Create a bookmark-sized form with space for the title of the book, its call number, and the collection alternatives: retain the book is to be retained, replace it with a new copy if available, replace it with a newer book, rebind it if it is out of print (remember that children don't seem to like rebound books and check them out less frequently), or withdraw and discard it.

Note the name of the book and its call number, and check the appropriate decision boxes on the slip. Put the slip into the book to let other staff know how to handle it.

Then you must act upon your decision:

If you have decided to retain the book, no further action is necessary.

If you want to replace the book with another copy of the same title, check *Books in Print* as to its availability and order it.

If you want to replace the book with a new title, check *Children's Catalog, Elementary School Library Collection,* or *The Horn Book Guide* for an appropriate title. Check that the replacement book is in print and order it.

If you want to rebind the book, send to bindery (but compare the cost of rebinding with the cost of a new book if available.)

If you want to remove the book, withdraw and discard it according to your library's procedure.

Building a Core Collection

While assessing your existing collection, you also need to be actively building a core collection of classics, basic books representing subject areas usually corresponding to the Dewey classifications, and some standard children's reference books.

Here again *Children's Catalog* and *Elementary School Library Collection* will help identify titles. If you have marked the library's holdings in one of these books, the process of identifying books in the core collection will go much more quickly. Other sources of core collection titles include *Best Books for Children* and *Best Books for Junior High.* The annual *Notable Children's Books* list selected by the ALSC Notable Children's Books Committee is published in the March 15 issue of *Booklist* and is also available on the Web at www.ala.org.

Buying New Books

Purchasing new books is usually the most interesting and rewarding part of collection development. All the skills and criteria developed for selecting adult materials will be used when looking at and reading reviews of juvenile materials. These criteria include:

1. The book's potential popularity and appeal.
2. The collection's need for the book's subject area. Some areas such as dinosaurs or holidays never seem to have enough titles, while others are more static.
3. The book's literary quality and effective writing.
   a. Nonfiction should be well organized, accurate, and up to date.
   b. Fiction should have good plot development and believable characters.
4. The book's format.
   a. Do the book's size and look fit its intended audience? For example, a few years back several adult short stories were published in picturebook format. These adult titles caused many headaches for catalogers, children's and adult services librarians, as they were not appropriate where they physically fit.
   b. Does the book have good illustrations appropriate to subject and age of potential reader? For example, books using licensed cartoon characters in their illustrations tend to miss the mark—children attracted by the cartoon characters are usually too young for the information, and students needing information typically discount material illustrated that way. Additionally, check illustra-

tions for accuracy; for example, is the ear of corn shown the same size as the head of wheat?

    c. Does the book have an index, table of contents, bibliography, pronunciation guides, and so on?

5. The book's accuracy and currency—is the information correct as far as you can determine (i.e., does a book on dinosaurs use the name *brontosaurus* or *apatosaurus?* Does a historical novel's setting appear authentic?)?

When choosing new books, remember to try for a variety of subjects from various viewpoints and reading levels. Also try to distribute the budget as fairly as possible (according to need) between fiction and nonfiction, and between new and replacement. Buying additional copies of very popular materials is well worthwhile. Also try to get multiples of anything you plan to booktalk to groups.

For more information about evaluating children's literature, see *From Cover to Cover: Evaluating and Reviewing Children's Books,* by Kathleen T. Horning (HarperCollins, 1997).

Nonprint Selection

Selecting nonprint materials may or may not be the responsibility of the children's librarian. If it is not, you should still be aware of the nonprint media budget and how it is allocated. You should scan reviews and make recommendations, suggestions, or wish lists for whomever does the purchasing.

When buying or suggesting videos, consider the aforementioned selection criteria as to quality, accuracy, and artistic merit. You must also be cognizant of public performance rights. Only videos for which the library owns public performance rights can be shown to groups in the library. Follow library policy on the purchase of full-length, recently released children's movies on video. Be aware that religious groups are also producing and promoting children's videos, and follow library policy on purchase of those items also. For parenting videos and other material designed for adults working with children, decide who purchases them and where to shelve them. For a quick summary of the best in children's video, be sure and read the list developed annually by the Notable Video Committee of ALSC. Another ALSC committee awards the Carnegie Medal for the most distinguished children's video released during the year.

Audiobooks are very popular. Young children love book-cassette combinations. These items are easy to promote to parents with the suggestion for in-car use. They are also excellent for making books a shared experience for families. Audiobooks of juvenile titles for older children are also popular. Unabridged audiobooks that follow a book word for word help older readers who may not read well develop some speed and facility by following along in the book. These titles also give you something to offer the visually impaired library user.

The ALSC Notable Recordings committee highlights the best in juvenile recordings in its annual Notable list. These cassettes and CDs fit in most libraries' collections very well.

Library policy on the purchase and use of materials in other formats, such as computer software, games, and informational CDs, should also be followed. If you want to start offering these materials, you must consider the library's mission, materials budget, availability of equipment to use and maintain these material formats, and their potential audience. Consider critical reviews of electronic materials and, if possible, try out the software itself before purchasing them. Remember that purchasing more board books may not be as splashy as buying a collection of computer games, but they may reach more children longer and may better suit the library's mission.

Replacement

Replacement is integral to the maintenance of a core collection. Systematic collection evaluation will see that worn, tired copies are replaced. Ask circulation staff to watch for damaged or worn books as well. Replacing these books is important because the impression they give is not inviting and will discourage the young library user.

If you don't have a library-wide method for replacing lost materials, try to set one up for the children's department. Consider purchasing duplicates or multiple copies of heavily used titles, both fiction and nonfiction. Multiple copies are especially helpful when you need to fill school assignment requests. Purchasing them is not out of line when you consider your library's policy on multiple copies of best-sellers.

The major difficulty in buying replacements is the fact that many titles go out of print so fast. You can be proactive by getting an additional copy of something very useful, but that is not always possible. If a title is out of print, look in prebinding company catalogs to see if it is still available as a prebound paperback. For something really important that is out of print, you can also consider an out-of-print search service. Several are available online, but be aware that there is typically an extra cost to search for an out-of-print title.

Good collection development is a delicate budgeting balance between the needs of the core collection, new materials, nonprint media, and replacements. It uses the skills you may have learned in a materials selection class and an awareness of the customers you serve. Information you will learn about the collection while evaluating it and purchasing for it also translates into better service for the children and adults using the collection.

7

Displays

One of the duties of a children's librarian is creating an environment that is inviting. One way to achieve this is through the use of interesting displays that are appropriate to the physical space of the children's area. In addition to creating an inviting space, displays can also be tools to promote the use of the children's collection, to define space, to promote activities, and to encourage children to use their own creativity. When developed for use outside the library, such as literature fairs and other community events, displays can also serve as an integral form of outreach.

In-Library Displays

Bulletin Boards

Bulletin boards are probably the most traditional form of in-library display. Most children's areas have at least one bulletin board—some have several. Decorating them (or delegating their decoration) falls to the children's librarian, who will need to decide or approve what to put on them.

How frequently a bulletin board is changed depends on the subject matter. Some displays have a seasonal or holiday theme and need to be changed accordingly. Other themes can stay up longer: one library created an eight-foot-tall millennium clock that counted down in months. The staff repositioned the hands each month and changed some small pictures around the clock.

You can create a long-lasting bulletin board theme that changes with the seasons. Use crumpled and flattened brown paper on a colored paper background to create a central background of leafless trees in springtime. Put green paper leaves on the tree branches for the summer. Replace them with colored paper leaves in the autumn, both on the trees and falling from them. For winter, show snowflakes falling on the trees and snow on the branches. Promote upcoming activities and events underneath the trees with characters, animals, and so on. Refresh the trees and colored background papers when they start to fade.

You may be fortunate enough to have entire walls that you can cover with display board, or you may have only a small bulletin board to create. In either case, the first thing you need to address is proportion. Large areas need large images, and small areas need smaller images.

You can size an image to a display area with an overhead projector. Use a photocopier to transfer the image to transparency film and project the image onto the display area. Adjust the image size with the projector (you may need to move the projector closer to or away from the display) until the projected image is the right size. Cover the display area with paper and trace the projected image.

You can use the resulting image to create string art images by stapling yarn along the lines. One librarian constructed four almost full-size string art horses galloping across a forty-foot wall of floor-to-ceiling bulletin board. Large tissue paper images were added for each season, such as butterflies in the summer, for example.

You can also divide a large bulletin board into more usable sections by using borders or a serial motif like a train with a series of boxcars or flat cars, each with a different cargo. Using segments works well with summer reading programs where you want to show participation by school or grade or week of program. They are also useful to promote a number of events.

Participation bulletin boards can be fun to watch as they grow weekly. For a storytime series theme of "Around the Farm," for example, you could begin with depicting a farmhouse, barn, garden, orchard, fields, and pond on the bulletin board. Then each week the children add something during storytime: apples to the orchard, ducks on the pond, laundry and a boa constrictor to the clothesline behind the farm house, and so on, depending on the stories.

If you have multiple bulletin boards, use one of them (or a section of one) as a monthly calendar of events. Make it big enough to be easily readable, and post programs, storytime themes, and trivia tidbits (National Pickle Week, for example—*Copycat* or *Chase's Calendar of Events* will give you ideas). This calendar is a very visual promotion, and parents especially will appreciate seeing the library's upcoming activities.

When you create bulletin boards, take advantage of the bulletin board materials available at teacher stores and some office supply stores. Cover a large space with color by stapling a thin plastic tablecloth (you can find them in many colors in party and paper goods supply stores) over the bulletin board. Judicious use of tiny holiday lights can really add panache, too. The images on greeting cards are another great source for bulletin board art. Enlarged to wall size, they can be breathtaking.

Tabletop Displays

The simplest tabletop display comprises a collection of books, either by a specific author or with a common theme, with a sign identifying them. You can easily dress up these displays by covering the table with a cloth, adding some covered boxes for different levels, and including some realia (a teddy bear in a rocker for bedtime stories, for example). Add clipboards with program sign-up sheets to display tables that promote an upcoming program.

Draw attention to tabletop displays. If you have a suspended tile ceiling, you can hang posters over the displays: use plant hangers and chains that fit over the suspending beams, and insert binder rings through the top of the poster and through the bottom link of the chain (lightweight poster board can even be held with bent paperclips and button thread).

Tabletop displays need to be changed more frequently than bulletin boards. Do not use anything irreplaceable in tabletop displays—display items will be handled and can get broken, or can easily be taken. Be sure to have enough books and materials to keep the table reasonably full, and alert the staff to restock with returned materials.

If you include handouts with a tabletop display, consider placement. For example, a bright-colored handout placed at the front of the display will be taken by three- and four-year-olds, even though it is a bibliography of middle-grade historical fiction titles. Put handouts toward the back of the display, but be sure display items don't obstruct them.

Case Displays

Display cases typically are lockable, so you can share small, fragile, or more valuable items, such as antique toys, bug collections, or paper sculpture with those who visit the library. Case displays are also more restrictive as to size, lighting, and location. Remember too that books used in display cases are not available for circulation.

Shelftop Displays

Children's areas are naturals for shelftop displays—the shelves are often lower and the shelftops are accessible. In the picture-book area, you can set books slightly opened, facing out. You can also display them at the end of each shelf.

Shelves in the juvenile area may have panels at the top, so you can add location signs (Biographies, Award Books, Children's Videos, etc.). Use a computer to design the sign in a large clear font, centered horizontally. Print the sign on heavy index-card weight paper. Trim it to a standard size, and attach it to a bookend with double-sided tape. Place the labeled bookend above the section.

Other Displays

You may want to consider some sort of interactive, in-library display. Freestanding cardboard boxes painted gray and taped together become excellent castle towers guarding the children's area entrance for the summer reading program. Add a blue cellophane moat, and a sheet of thin plywood painted brown and attached to the towers with plastic chain to complete the castle effect. Space capsules made from refrigerator and other large appliance boxes are also fun.

One enterprising library made a series of child-sized cardboard figures without heads. These figures were available for photo opportunities, where the children stood behind the figures with their necks and heads showing above them. The resulting pictures were great fun.

Suspended ceilings are great for hanging displays of lightweight items. Use bent paper clips, tape, and heavy-duty thread to hang a series of silhouettes over the biographies or paper fish over the reading area. Because air currents can cause these displays to move, be sure they will not trigger motion detector alarms your library may have.

Mannequins also make interesting display items. Make a scarecrow to sit in the corner of the children's room in the fall. A giant Paul Bunyan figure of papier mache and chicken wire in the lobby can hold a card proclaiming a "Tall Tale Travels" program. Later, you can spray him with silver paint, add a helmet, and make him a spaceman. Use green paint and a Halloween wig and make him an alien.

Sometimes a library's children's area is given large creations by schoolchildren and Scouts, such as a six-foot-tall Clifford the Big Red Dog made from papier mache, or an entire Little Town on the Prairie constructed of cardboard, foam core, and sticks. If you have the space, you can host these creations for a while, but be sure the donors know that you accept them with no guarantees and at a certain point you will need to dispose of them.

Out-of-Library Displays

You may be asked to represent the library with a display at a reading fair, children's health fair, Scout leadership meeting, expectant and new parent conference, or other community youth-focused event. These functions can also be considered outreach.

When you are asked to attend a function of this type, be sure to find out

the name and phone number of the contact person

exact location (including street address, floor, and room name), doors to enter by

where to park and if there will be a loading area

the time span of event and when you need to be set up by

the display table size, if it will be covered, and number of chairs provided

the expected audience size and ages

any event-specific handout requested

Display Supplies

What you take to a display should vary only in appropriateness for the audience. After doing dozens of displays for events over the years, I recommend getting a couple of collapsible luggage carts with large wheels and long bungee cords for rolling up display materials; two to four plastic milk crates for packing the display materials and books and then creating multilevel displays; clear acrylic sign holders, folding bookstands, bookends, masking tape, rubber bands, and scissors.

Also take decorative stickers in rolls or sheets. I use old summer reading program stickers, offering them to children walking by. I can then approach the parents to tell them about the library. By keeping track of the sticker backing paper, I can estimate how many families I've spoken to. I know I have already talked to the parents if I see their children already have stickers.

An adjustable wheeled chair is also useful both as a comfortable, solid chair to sit on, which is not always provided, and to roll heavy boxes of books. You also might want to take a table cover, such as an old quilt or an inexpensive lightweight plastic or fabric tablecloth.

Even though most events provide name signs, I always display a large two-foot by three-foot vinyl banner (purchased at a local sign shop) with my library's name and logo on it. A library's logo on a kite that expands easily also can work well.

Having something to give those who stop at your display is good business. Bring bibliographies that are appropriate to the event's audience, calendars of events, bookmarks with the library's address and hours, a map to show exactly where the library is located, and library card applications. A list of great children's web sites is always welcome. Bring handouts from other departments that are appropriate. At an event for teachers, I bring indexes and professional materials they may not be aware of but would find useful. Remove all rubber bands from your handouts, unless it is very windy and you are outside, as most people will not take things banded together.

I bring only a few display books and materials, more for an example of what the library offers than to use. I choose books with bright covers and popular appeal as well as some sample videos and CDs to display.

Bring free plastic bookbags if your library provides them. Keep them under the table to hand out, one per family to limit them. If your library doesn't provide bookbags, bring some plastic grocery bags to give to people with their hands full.

Display Activities

While staffing a display at a community event, you may be asked to provide an activity for children who visit your table. You can use this activity to promote the resources of the library and help personalize library service for those you meet. Children always remember doing an activity as well as having something to take home with them.

A simple yet effective activity is using rubber stamps and markers to make bookmarks. Bring index card weight paper cut into bookmark-width strips, a box of rubber stamps, and washable ink pads and markers, and let the kids create. I punch a hole in one end of the marker and add a yarn loop. If you are asked to provide something related to the event, you can supply a coloring sheet for the children to take home.

At a book festival with hundreds of touring school children, I devised six 12" x 18" fractured fairy-tale cards to quiz the students. The fairy-tale scenes shown on the cards each had something wrong in them. I showed the card and asked the children first what fairy tale was depicted and then what was wrong. For example, one card showed a picture of three goats and a bridge but under the bridge was a dolphin wearing a crown, not a troll. If a group knew all the answers, I gave its teacher or chaperone a poster from a past summer reading program and a bundle of bookmarks to distribute later. This activity works very well for a group, as no lining up or turn waiting is involved.

Interest Getters

You can add interest to a display table full of bibliographies, books, and small signs encouraging people to come to storytime and to visit the library web site. I have a collection of book character dolls, foam rubber rocks, and large plastic bugs and lizards. These items (especially the bugs and lizards) get the children to stop and look at the table. They also hold the children's attention fairly well while I talk to their parents.

8

Bibliographies and Booktalks

Bibliographies

Producing and distributing bibliographies can be very helpful to children's librarians. They are especially useful where there is limited specialized department staffing and where the library does a lot of outreach.

Bibliographies help guide children and adults through the maze of available juvenile materials. Children's bibliographies can range from a simple list of preprimer titles for the child just learning to read or a list of regional children's authors all the way to an extensive annotated listing of juvenile historical fiction by eras.

When creating a bibliography, whether short or lengthy, you should outline and follow some criteria for selecting the titles to include. While it goes without saying that you will include titles from lists of recommended books, other things need to be considered, such as number of copies owned, the condition and currency of the titles, and the audience of the bibliography.

One of my criteria for including a title in a bibliography is that a minimum of eight copies are available among my system's twenty-nine branches. Unless your library is a single facility, directing everyone to the same single copy is not good service. I also check the status of those copies at the time I am making up the bibliography. If two or more are noted as lost, I don't include the title. I check the title's condition, although I cannot check multiple copies. If I am pulling together a sample exhibit from the bibliography, I take only those in good shape.

Sorting by age appropriateness is also important for a bibliography, even if the designation is just a general "For Younger Readers" or "For Older Readers." Adults using the list to find books for their children will know they are in the right area.

Types of Bibliographies

Some bibliographies should be readily available, such as lists of state children's reading award nominees and national award-winning books. ALA's *Guide to Best Reading* each year is a convenient source of copy-ready masters for these bibliographies.

Other bibliographies are also useful. A bibliography for parents on selecting appropriate books for their children, a list of state authors of children's books, a list of books set within a state, and lists of books comparable to popular books ("If you like . . . you will also like. . .") can all be helpful. Other bibliographic topics that are popular with parents include listings by grade, lists of good read-alouds, lists of books for family activities, and lists of books to help parents and children get through trying times.

Grade-level lists give a parent or grandparent some idea of where to look when there is no reader's advisor available. Preparing lists by grade may disturb some librarians and teachers. You can solve that dilemma by making these lists relatively long (more than seventy-five titles) and noting that the suggested titles include a range of difficulty to accommodate both the difference in reading ability among children within a grade and to accommodate the development of reading skills during the school year.

Several different "trying times" lists can be prepared that are also helpful to parents or grandparents. In bookmark or half-sheet format, list eight to twelve titles, both fiction and nonfiction if available, dealing with such subjects as adapting to a new sibling or being afraid of the dark. Titles for these bibliographies are listed by subject in the indexes of *The Bookfinder*, *Children's Catalog*, *Best Books for Children*, and *A to Zoo*.

Many of the bibliographies I do are request-driven. The 4-H club requested a list of books that portrayed positive character traits. For the 4-H request, I printed only a few copies for in-library use and gave the 4-H leader an original master so that she could make as many copies as she needed. When Girl Scout leaders asked for silly songs, I created a short list of silly song books. As time permits, you can also create bibliographies based on your personal interest or as a result of a branch request.

When preparing bibliographies for children, especially for those in the middle grades, I tend to do more author lists than title lists. This breakdown gives wider availability and can encourage the readers to read more books by authors they've enjoyed. Bibliographies of mysteries, adventure, sports, and humor are easily done this way.

While not bibliographies, strictly speaking, lists of good children's web sites are also very useful. They can promote what is of value and appropriate for young people on the Web and can help them develop their web skills. Lists of web sites can familiarize a reader with authors or illustrators and their work. ALSC maintains "700+ Great Sites; Amazing, Spectacular, Mysterious, Wonderful Web Sites for Kids and the Adults Who Care about Them" (www.ala.org/parentspage/greatsites/amazing.html). Parents, too, often find these sites a useful way to explore books.

Another type of bibliography is the pathfinder. These lists cover nonfiction subjects and provide information about research resources. They list reference sources, databases, search engine web headings, and subject headings. Pathfinders for science fair projects or the ubiquitous "state notebook" topics are invaluable.

For ideas for bibliographies and recommended titles, search other library's web sites and join a children's literature on-line discussion group. Take some of your latest bibliographies to meetings of other children's librarians and ask them to share theirs with you. When you attend the ALA Annual Conference, visit LAMA's PR Swap and Shop. There are always some great handouts there to jump start ideas.

At the bottom of the bibliography, add pertinent subject headings where other titles can be found. Always date your bibliographies, and include your department, the name of your library, and your library's Web address. You can also include pertinent web sites on your bibliographies.

Bibliography Format

Bibliographies are fairly easy to produce and update with ordinary word processing computer software. Use a clear font in an easy-to-read size. An added benefit of producing bibliographies on a networked computer is that the library's webmaster can easily retrieve them and post them on the library's web site. Your bibliographies can thus be available electronically.

If you use computer generated graphics to decorate the bibliographies, don't manipulate the images to the point that they are unrecognizable. Copyright-free clip art is readily available on CD-ROM or in book form.

Be sure to request and receive permission to use graphics that are under copyright. To use an illustration or to reproduce anything exactly from a book, you need to contact the publisher's rights and permissions office. When permission is granted, you will be sent a formal acknowledgement statement, such as "Used with permission," that typically must appear with the image.

You need to get permission to use the Newbery and Caldecott medals. To use these images, you must write to the ALA Office of Rights and Permissions and specify how you want to use them. The use of the medals' images, like many ALA materials, would be free for educational, nonprofit purposes. For a small fee you can also purchase camera-ready art of the medals. You can telephone the ALA Office of Rights and Permissions at (800) 545-2433, ext. 5103, or fax to (312) 944-8741.

Take margins and fold space into account when you format a bibliography. I have standardized bibliography formats after talking with my printer. The standard format helps in storage as well as display, because quantities of similar sizes are easier to deal with and lay out attractively.

You can also standardize print quantities. If you send the bibliographies out to be commercially printed, find out about minimum quantities and lead time. While large print runs may be less expensive per piece, consider the life span of the information and decide quantity accordingly. If you have access to high-speed photocopying, you can print a few copies at a time to have on hand; you can also quickly provide updated bibliographies.

Booktalks

Booktalks are verbal annotations, or "commercials," to encourage someone to read a book that you have read and enjoyed. Booktalks can range from brief two or three sentences, comparable to the annotations in the Notable Children's Books lists, to four to five paragraphs, such as a newspaper review column. You can present spontaneous booktalks as you walk through the children's department by making suggestions to a child, or you can present a formal thirty-minute program to a group of fifth graders on a class visit to the library.

Reader's advisory work is frequently booktalking. You mention titles of books that might fit children's requests and tell them a bit more about titles you are personally familiar with.

Joni Bodart literally wrote the book about booktalking. While most of her five books are for young adults and adults, her process works well for children's booktalks, too. In *Booktalk!2,* she details her method in preparing and presenting booktalks. Her two unbreakable rules are: don't tell the ending, and don't talk about books you haven't read. There are good reasons for these rules—not telling the ending means the children have to read the book to find out what happens, and if you booktalk only books you have read, you won't get blindsided by an unanswerable question.

Some publishers provide booktalks for their books. These prepared booktalks are free and can be sent to you via e-mail. Visit publishers' web sites for prepared booktalks (and a host of additional information) and to subscribe to their e-mail lists. Although the prepared booktalks don't absolve you from having to read the book, they will save time in trying to decide what points of the book to stress.

Like Joni Bodart, I recommend preparing notecards with pertinent information—author, title, characters' names, a very brief plot summary, and page numbers of good sections to read aloud. I mark these pages in the book with paperclips to easily find them during the booktalk.

When I do formal booktalks, I like to group the books by types or historic era. These groupings work well for booktalking state award nominated children's books to staff working with children. I use this booktalking assignment to encourage staff to read the nominees on their own time so that they can recommend appropriate titles to children. In my state, for example, twenty books are nominated for the state award. I select one of each type for a more in-depth booktalk with the staff and mention in passing the other titles that are also dog stories or set during the Civil War. I also call the staff's attention to parts of a book that may be controversial or to the particular strengths of a book.

If I am booktalking books of my own selection (not responding to a particular request for certain types of books), I try to choose an eclectic range of books, both new and old, that go together thematically such as *Susan and*

Her Classic Convertible, The Beetle and Me, and *Chitty Chitty Bang Bang,* which are all books with cars. These booktalks introduce today's young readers to good books they may be overlooking, and they also spread out requests for individual books.

You can also use themes to mix nonfiction with fiction, and picture books with the chapter books. Consider, for example, booktalking *Children of the Dust Bowl, Out of the Dust, Treasures in the Dust, Blue Willow, Potato,* and *The Gardener* together.

Try mixing some of the recent biographies and picture biographies of Americans in a booktalk, too. A booktalk of the following titles would likely interest a wide range of ages, including grandparents: *Snowflake Bentley, Bill Peet, Eleanor, The Story of Ruby Bridges, Wilma Unlimited, Boss of the Plains, Always Inventing, Small Steps, Knots in My Yo-Yo String, Minty: The Story of the Young Harriet Tubman,* and *Molly Bannaky.*

When I booktalk, I save reading aloud from the book for only the books I like best. For example, when talking about *Missing May* by Cynthia Rylant, I set the stage by reading from the very beginning where Summer explains about love and recognizing it.

Sample Booktalk

Silent to the Bone, by E. L. Konigsburg; 2000, Atheneum

SIAS—summarize in a sentence. But how can Connor summarize what's happening to his best friend, Branwell, who sits in traumatized muteness in the Behavior Center, accused of harming his baby sister? Would the boy who tried too hard to be the perfect son and grandson regain the ability to speak in time to save himself? Can Connor discover enough of the truth to help? *Silent to the Bone:* SIAS.

A gripping read about friendship, infatuation, possessiveness, understanding, and ultimately love.

Books for Booktalking

Butterworth, W. E.
Susan and Her Classic Convertible
Four Winds, 1970

Cochrane, Patricia
Purely Rosie Pearl
Delacorte, 1996

Fleming, Ian
Chitty Chitty Bang Bang
Aeonian, 1976

Gates, Doris
Blue Willow
Puffin, 1976

Hesse, Karen
Out of the Dust
Scholastic, 1997

Lied, Kate
*Potato: A Tale from the Great
   Depression*
National, 1997

Porter, Tracy
Treasures in the Dust
HarperCollins, 1997

Stanley, Jerry
Children of the Dust Bowl
Crown, 1992

Stewart, Sarah
The Gardener
Farrar, 1997

Turner, Ann
Dust for Dinner
HarperCollins, 1995

Young, Karen
The Beetle and Me
Greenwillow, 1999

9

Library Instruction, Tours, and Outreach

Library Instruction

Library skills are best taught in sequenced instruction. In many areas school libraries may be uneven, and the public library serves as the main resource library for homeschooled children. Sometimes, library skills are presented collaboratively by school and public libraries. The school library's focus is curriculum support, while your instruction on using the public library also should support intellectual curiosity, intellectual freedom, and inquiry.

It is helpful to have an idea of the sequences involved in helping children learn to use the library effectively. The following guide should help you know what is appropriate to introduce and when to introduce it. These are general guidelines only. Of course, while these skills are considered appropriate for the stated ages, never assume that children have had this instruction. Remember that each child achieves skills at his or her own pace. Finally, remember to encourage children of all ages to ask the librarian for help and suggestions.

> The preschool-kindergarten aged child should be familiar with the library and the librarian and know that there are a variety of materials available. She is aware of appropriate library behavior and follows library procedures and rules. She knows how to handle books and knows the difference between an author and an illustrator.

A first grader has his own library card, can find different sections in the library—adult, picture books, juvenile nonfiction and understands that books are arranged in order and that they should be kept that way. He can alphabetize by first letter, identify parts of a book, and understands the difference between fiction and nonfiction.

Second graders are able to locate fiction books by the author's last name and understand that nonfiction books are arranged by the Dewey Decimal System (or those numbers on the back). They can select books on specific subjects of interest and have been introduced to picture book award winning books.

A third grader can use the online catalog to find books. He knows where to find the reference collection and can look things up in the encyclopedia. He has been told about plagiarism, intellectual property rights, and the necessity of putting information in his own words rather than copying directly out of the book. He selects his books very carefully, having definite opinions on what he wants to read, knows the parts of a title page—title, author and illustrator, and is moving into chapter books and genre reading.

The fourth grade student should be able to locate materials by call number and biographies by the last name of the subject of the book. She can be introduced to other reference sources, such as an almanac, an atlas, a CD-ROM, the Internet, and the thesaurus. She will use the index to find articles in the encyclopedia and is able to use the online catalog independently, interpreting its information to be able to find it if it is available. She knows more genres—mystery, science fiction, historical fiction, biographies and recognizes and understands the significance of more award books—Newbery, Coretta Scott King and her state award.

Fifth graders should be able to choose between several reference sources to identify the most appropriate. They can use cross references and primary source material. They can put together a simple bibliography.

Sixth graders have grasped the concept of the Dewey Decimal System and know its 10 major sections and numbers for some specific topics. They can search by subject and convert their own terms into appropriate subject headings. They are learning the difference between subject and keyword searching and are starting to develop search strategies for searching online, the periodical index, and the Internet. They are gravitating towards the Young Adult area.

Seventh and eighth graders know to use the tracings on the online catalog for alternate subject headings. They search more in detail with keywords. They can develop more detailed bibliographies and have branched out to use online databases and various search engines to find additional information. They are starting to discriminate between search engines and internet sites for usefulness, accuracy and appropriateness.

The high school student is aware there are special libraries—medical, science, law, etc., and special collections within the library—local history, genealogy, business. He can transfer search skills from one search system to another and can evaluate all materials for accuracy, appropriateness and usefulness. He uses special reference sources: literary criticism, poetry, and play indexes. He uses the adult as well as the young adult collection and reads classics as well as contemporary titles.

Library Tours and Class Visits

School and class visits come in several permutations, from in-library and in-school visits to informational and program-related visits. Each type takes slightly different preparation on your part.

Strongly encourage teachers to schedule in-library visits well ahead of time. When teachers contact you to schedule an in-library visit, ask about the number of children, the grade level, and the length of the visit. You will also want to ask these questions: Is the visit for a library tour or for a story program? Will the students be doing research? Will they be checking out books? How many books will each child be allowed to check out? Will the children have their own library cards, or will the teacher use a class library card? Have arrangements been made for children who don't have library cards?

You may run into unannounced in-library visits. Have a contingency plan for these visits. Directions to an area the group can use and a prepared sheet of information about scheduling in-library visits can be handed to the teacher with these groups. Any planned, scheduled programs will take precedence over unannounced visits, which will need to wait their turn.

You may also be asked to make in-school class or school visits. Find out your library's policy on in-school visits so that you know how to respond. Some libraries do not provide in-school entertainment visits, but other libraries consider them to be a form of public relations and library promotion. Some libraries allow them only in conjunction with promoting a library program such as the Summer Reading Program or for Library Career talks.

As with in-library visits, in-school visits should be scheduled ahead of time. Here again, you need to ask the teacher some questions, such as the purpose of your visit, what grades you will be visiting, how many students are involved, how long your presentation should be, and where the presentation will take place (classroom, gym, or auditorium?). You will want to find out practical matters, too, such as where you should park, and if you need to sign in at the office.

One very useful, cooperative in-school visit uses the school's computer lab to instruct students how to use the library's online catalog and even how to access their library card account. Few public libraries have adequate terminals to teach this information in a group or lab setting.

One library taught all the fourth graders in a school how to use the library's online catalog and library card accounts over a four-day period of in-school visits. Three students were assigned to each terminal, with the fastest keyboarder at the keyboard. Two adults helped the groups of students while the librarian presented the program.

The visit used a dummy library card account to teach students how they could access their own accounts. The account showed what books were checked out on the card and if any fines were outstanding. In response to this class, the other teachers in the school asked the library to repeat the class for them.

Outreach

Displays, participation on local boards and committees, and public speaking are all outreach responsibilities of a children's librarian. Other outreach activities include radio and television appearances and contest judging. Out-of-library displays are discussed in Chapter 7.

Your participation on boards and committees can vary from active membership within a community child advocacy committee to attending a brainstorming session to help a group write a grant. While these activities can be time consuming, they are also valuable opportunities to network, cooperate, and disseminate information about the library and its services.

More frequently than almost any other department of the library, with the possible exception of genealogy, children's librarians are asked to speak to groups about the library and what it has to offer children and their parents. They are also asked to talk about new children's books and publishing trends for children and storytelling. Requests for these programs come from parent and teacher groups, women's groups, child care and other professional associations, mothers' clubs, educators, vocational child care classes, and teen parenting classes.

While the prospect of giving one of these programs may be daunting, you will find them actually very easy, because people love being read to. A sample talk to a parent group and a talk about storytelling appear at the end of this chapter.

When asked to do a talk, find out the exact location: street address, room name, where to park, and what doors to enter by. Clarify if you will be speaking before or after a business meeting, meal, or other session, and when the program will start. Also ask if any special area should be stressed, such as award books, parenting materials, or the value of reading aloud for child brain development. Ask how long you should plan to speak.

Ask how many people are expected and if children will in the audience as well as adults. If the group is large, or the program is being held in a gym, ask about a sound system. An audience that cannot hear you will soon lose interest, and projecting your voice to a large group or room can be very exhausting. If a sound system is not available at the facility but you have access to one, bring it along.

Find out your library's policy for payment for speaking. My library expects library staff to refuse payment for speaking, offering compensatory time instead. These programs are considered outreach and part of the library's service to the community. Staff at my library are allowed to keep the small speakers' gifts sometimes given by groups, such as candles, bath salts or hand lotion, and the occasional bookstore gift certificate.

A Sample Parent Group Talk

Following is a fully developed piece. You may want to use all or part of it. You can adapt it to your own collection and style of presentation.

CHOOSING AND SHARING BOOKS WITH YOUR CHILDREN

Following your introduction, step up to the mike, smile, and greet your audience. Add any additional information you think the group should know about you, and begin:

"Good evening! I am glad to be here tonight because it gives me an opportunity to share with you something I believe is very important—sharing books and stories with your children. I am going to start by sharing one with you."

At this point, read aloud a surefire picture book, showing the pictures as you do. Draw attention to the Caldecott seal and mention that the book was recognized for its distinguished pictures. Tops and Bottoms *by Janet Stevens or* Owl Moon *by Jane Yolen are both good introductory books. If you enjoy storytelling instead of reading aloud, you could tell "The Tailor" (the introductory story in* Just Enough to Make a Story *by Nancy Schimmel).*

Then move on to what the library has to offer:

"The library offers many activities and a wealth of material for the whole family. For adults there are book discussion groups, special programs, and a wide ranging collection with everything from the latest bestseller to information on how to install a water heater or plan a budget vacation. And for your children there is even more. The library offers storytimes *[mention your library's days and times]*, children's programs such as *[mention some past and upcoming programs, and the appropriate age levels]*, children's book discussion groups *[give the titles of previously discussed and future books]*, and of course the summer reading program, to help children develop into lifelong learners who read for enjoyment and to maintain their reading skills over the summer."

Read another book, such as Mushroom in the Rain *by Mirra Ginsburg or a version of* There Was an Old Lady Who Swallowed a Fly. *Instead, you could tell a participation story at this point, such as "The King with the Terrible Temper" from* With a Deep Sea Smile *by Virginia Tashijian.*

"When parents visit the library, they are often overwhelmed by the sheer numbers of books available and want help in finding the right book. When your child is very young, check out the Mother Goose rhymes, children's songbooks, and books of finger plays. Read, sing, and share these with your arm and lap babies."

Hold up examples of these books, and if there is time lead the
group in a finger play.

"As your lap baby becomes a toddler, look for books with simple clear pictures that are easy to 'read' and focus on—short stories that reflect your child's world and books you won't mind rereading over and over. Check out the library's collection of board books for this age child. If your child does have a favorite, you might consider purchasing it or suggest purchasing it to Grandma. Then it will be available to be a friendly comfort for your child when she's not feeling well or he's sleeping away from home."

Hold up examples of these books. If time allows or the audience is
mostly parents of preschool children, read Ten Nine Eight *by Molly*
Bang or Goodnight Moon *by Margaret Wise Brown.*

"For your preschooler, select books that compliment your child's character. *A Is for Annabelle* by Tasha Tudor is perfect for a quiet daughter, while a rambunctious son might prefer *The Snowy Day* by Ezra Jack Keats. Consider if the book will answer your child's questions or raise more. Are the pictures worth looking at? Could you read it over and over? Simple concept books about colors, shapes, and the letters of the alphabet can be shared as well as children's poetry."

Hold up examples, and if time allows, read one, or read
a humorous poem.

"A five-year-old has a much wider vocabulary and interests. Capitalize on these by widening the variety of books you select. Extend the story by asking your child to retell it from the pictures or to draw his own pictures to go with the story. Start sharing the classic fairy tales, but be sure to check endings so that you have versions you are comfortable with. Bedtime is too late to realize that you've got a version where the wolf is chowing down on a pork dinner rather then chasing the pigs to the third little pig's house. Use the children's nonfiction collection for well-illustrated books about animals, birds and bugs. They will be found in the 500s."

*Hold up examples, and show some pages of an easy
nonfiction book.*

"Your kindergartner and first grader will want variety and lots of easy-to-read books. Continue to read aloud to your new readers. Children's listening vocabulary is much larger than their reading vocabulary, and reading aloud continues this mutually enjoyable routine. Look for books you can read together because of their repetition. *Alexander and the Terrible, Horrible, No Good Very Bad Day* by Judith Viorst is a good example of this kind of book, as is *Green Eggs and Ham* by Dr. Seuss."

Hold up examples, and read Alexander *if time allows.*

"As your children become independent readers, encourage them by allowing them to choose their own books. Suggest they read others by an author they liked but make reading an option, not required. Realize that children who read series books are getting reading practice, which is important. While series books are formulaic and seldom literary masterpieces, they do give the young reader a sense of accomplishment, the security of familiarity and an opportunity to read for pleasure. As they mature they will move on to other books and types of books. How many of you still read Nancy Drew or the Hardy Boys? Discuss what your children are reading and share with them the kinds of books you like to read.

"Encourage juvenile nonfiction reading—joke and craft books, pets and poetry—and biographies."

Hold up examples of these books, and if time allows, read
The Glorious Flight *by Martin and Alice Provensen.*

"The library offers other services *[mention those that are appropriate and add any that weren't mentioned earlier]* to help your child and you. Our web site offers access to our catalog so that you can research what's available and place holds from home. It will also let you know at which branch the book is on the shelf for emergency pickup. There's an area of homework help with databases available for searching. Our children's web page offers fun child appropriate links, craft and activity ideas and coloring pages.

"Choosing and sharing books with your children are easy ways to raise readers. Jim Trelease, author of *The New Read Aloud Handbook*, recommends a reading light by every bed and a book shelf in every bathroom. I want to recommend a library card for every child, a regular day to visit the library, and a special place in the home to keep the library books because it has been shown that children learn from example and where parents read and make a special place for books in their lives and home, children will also.

"The next-to-the-last thing I want to share with you is a stanza often quoted by children's librarians from 'The Reading Mother' by Strickland Gillian."

> You may have tangible wealth untold,
>
> Caskets of jewels and coffers of gold,
>
> richer than I you can never be,
>
> I had a mother who read to me.

"And finally, I would like to close with *The Very Quiet Cricket* by Eric Carle."

Read The Very Quiet Cricket *(be sure to get one that still chirps).*

"There are handouts on the table over there. Are there any questions?"

A Sample Program about Storytelling

The following sample program is a presentation for parents, teachers, or childcare-givers.

CREATIVE STORY TELLING AND SHARING BOOKS WITH CHILDREN

Following your introduction, greet the audience, and share any additional information you think the group should know about you.

Smile and start by telling "The Tailor" from Just Enough to Make a Story *by Nancy Schimmel. This beginning is excellent because it lays the ground for the rest of the program.*

"Now I would like to know a little bit about you. How many of you work directly with children? With children only under two? Between two and four? Four and six? Seven and over? Mixed ages? I will try and share with you ideas, books, and materials you can take back and use immediately.

"While the uses of story are many, I want to talk about their ability to educate and entertain. Teaching through story is not new. In fact there is strong precedence set for its value. And we all know that everyone loves a good story."

Read Tops and Bottoms *by Janet Stevens, holding it up*
so all can see the pictures.

"Of course, in order for a story to educate as well as entertain, it must be appropriate for its audience. A trickster tale like *Tops and Bottoms* with its allusion to the fable of the Tortoise and the Hare would be appropriate for just about everyone over three years old, and some two-year-olds would probably get the joke too. Stories with the themes of sharing and kindness for example work well with a wide age range while others need to be grown into. *Glorious Flight: Across the Channel with Louis Bleriot* by Alice and Martin Provensen, for example, is a beautifully illustrated history of flight and biography of Louis Bleriot. It won the Caldecott Medal as the most distinguished American picture book for children of the year it was published. Nevertheless, it is a book for fourth graders, not four-year-olds."

Read Glorious Flight *aloud to the group.*

"Books must not only be developmentally appropriate by theme and content, they need to be the right length—not too long, not too short, but just right—and have the right intensity. Some books and stories have an intensity to them that is frightening to our seemingly worldly children. For children raised on the first pig and the second pig finding safety with the third pig, the version where the wolf consumes the first two pigs and in turn is consumed by the third can be a scary shock. Of course, to some four- and five-year-old boys, it can be, finally, the right version. Your knowledge of the children in your care can help you make the right choice."

Read The True Story of the Three Little Pigs as Told by
A. Wolf *by John Sciezcka.*

"When you want to tell stories, there are lots of sources available to you. Primarily, there is your memory. All of you, I am certain, could tell a credible 'Goldilocks and the Three Bears,' 'Three Billy Goats Gruff,' or 'Three Little Pigs.' And there are collections of stories suitable for telling. My favorite is *I'll Tell You a Story, I'll Sing You a Song* by Christine Allison. This book, subtitled *A Parent's Guide to the Fairy Tales, Fables, Songs, and Rhymes of Childhood,* is a treasure trove of storylines with special sections on how to light a story, make up your own stories, and alternative endings. It also has sections of fables with the moral spelled out on the bottom, the words to many children's songs—we can remember the tune but after Jimmy cracked that corn what did he do?—and Mother Goose rhymes and finger plays. I often recommend it as a wonderful baby present or the perfect flood book for a camp counselor. Caroline Bauer's *New Handbook for Storytellers* is another useful, adaptable resource. These, and other resources and indexes are available at the library."

Hold up the books.

"If you are selecting books to read aloud to your children, there is a very useful book you should know about, *A to Zoo: Subject Access to Children's Picture Books* in the reference area of the library. You want to choose books that are big enough to be seen, books with plenty of white space or color or design qualities that make them suitable for sharing. And, of course, books with great stories. Be sure to hold the book up where the children can see it.

"This one is a favorite of three- and four-year-olds."

Read Old Black Fly *by Jim Aylesworth.*

"There are other ways of storytelling besides the traditional telling. Consider telling using a flannel board or with puppets."

Show and tell a flannel board story. Pass around a story piece you've made from Pellon interfacing and colored with crayons. Ahead of time, make stick puppets for the characters in "The Little Red Hen" using die-cut shapes or clip art drawings for the hen, chicks, dog, cat, and pig taped to straws or craft sticks. Distribute these to audience members and have them raise their puppets when their character is mentioned.

"Play acting and participation stories are also fun and help get the children involved in the story. Jack Kent's *Fat Cat* is fun to act out with a sheet and an axe made from a paper tube and paper blade. Children play the parts of the consumed neighbors by hiding under the sheet draped in front of you. Children also like to act out classics like 'Three Billy Goats Gruff' or 'The Enormous Turnip.'"

"Finally, don't forget story and song and story and poetry. 'The Old Woman Who Swallowed a Fly,' for example, is a story, a song, and a play all together. And there is a wealth of children's poetry available to drop into a quiet moment.'"

Hold up examples of picture songbooks and children's poetry collections.

"Children are young for a very short time in the scheme of their lives. Using story to educate and entertain them will enrich their childhoods and give them memories to grow on.'"

"On the table is a tip sheet on learning stories to tell and a list of the books and resources I have shared with you today. The library has many more support materials, including flannel board pattern books, *[discuss here highlights of your collection and services]* and don't forget that you can access the library catalog on the Web and place holds in the comfort of your home or office. And our *[insert name of children's web area]* has lots of craft and project ideas. Are there any questions? Then I would like to finish with one last story.'"

Read or tell a personal favorite story.

Children's Library Web Sites

A good children's web page is a special form of outreach. It can promote your programs, services, and collection, entertain young folks, inform their parents, and more! If your library does not have a children's web page, suggest its development. Features of a notable public library children's department web site include:

Bibliographies: by genre, age level, and subject

Homework-related links and children's search engines

An "ask a question" feature

Parenting links

Children's crafts and activities

Internet safety guidelines

Calendar of library programs and events

Local youth entertainment guide

Suggestion form

Acquisition suggestion form

Interactive reading games

Online games

Virtual library tour

Gallery of children's art and projects

Links to children's book and author sites

10

Issues and Challenges

Children's librarians face some issues and challenges that are unique to working with children. No one worries if a scientific treatise in the adult nonfiction collection is age-appropriate for its reader, for example, yet many people are concerned about age appropriateness of materials for children. If hours of service must be cut, some will suggest that the children's area should bear the brunt, saying children's information needs are not as important as adult needs. Open Internet access for children is a large challenge, especially from those who want to "protect" children but who may not realize that filters can be unreliable and lead to a false sense of security. And children themselves are challenging in all their marvelous stages and diversity.

Access

Access, for children's library service, covers a range of areas. Access issues may be internal or external to the library. External issues—school hours, traffic patterns, and library building location, for example—are almost always beyond the control of the librarian. Even so, you should be aware they exist and take them into account when developing internal access guidelines.

Internal access issues involve the collection, library hours, services (interlibrary loan, reference, and reader's advisory), the Internet, and space.

Children should have equal access to the children's collection and to the adult collection, although parents may impose and enforce limits for their own children (but only their own children).

In terms of library hours, the children's area should be open the same hours as the rest of the library.

Interlibrary loan, reference, and reader's advisory assistance, as well as all other services provided by the library, should be equally available to children and adults. In fact, children are less likely to ask for help. When they do ask, children's staff should make an extra effort to completely and thoroughly answer their questions.

Access to Internet terminals should be proportionately equal for children and adults if the terminals are located away from the children's area in a separate part of the building. The same acceptable use policy should govern both adults and children. Consider restricting the use of the terminals in the children's area, identifying them as "children only" or "child and parent only." Alternatively, you might institute a policy that allows adult use only when no child is waiting to use these terminals.

The children's area should also be accessible to children with mobility handicaps. While ramps, curb cuts, and automatic doors are as much a boon to parents with strollers and toddlers as they are to folks in wheelchairs, it is important to be in compliance with the law and welcoming to all children.

Privacy

The young library user has the same right to privacy in his reading selections as the adult library. Parents concerned about what their children check out should visit the library with them. They should also stay with their children to help in their selections.

Children's library staff should not presume to know what kinds of books parents want their children to read. Parents should discuss with their children what is appropriate for their family; the parents must then enforce those limits. The library has no authority (or desire) to monitor what individual children are reading.

Sometimes a child's right to privacy conflicts with a parent's need to know, especially when there is a missing book involved. If the missing book is checked out on the child's card, suggest to the parent that the child call the library for the name of the book, or have the child look it up in the account section on the library's web site. If keeping track of books that are checked out is a continuing problem for a family, suggest that the parent check the family's books out on the parent's card for a single record.

Age Appropriateness

This book has stressed the importance of age appropriateness for children's materials. Books too easy or too difficult will not satisfy young readers, and books too sophisticated will shortchange them.

Presenting and promoting age appropriate materials can be difficult. Parents, proud that their second grader has sixth-grade reading skills, may insist you suggest sixth-grade level materials. For these children, try suggesting children's classics, like *The Wind in the Willows* or *The Wonderful Wizard of Oz*. Classics like these don't deal with the contemporary issues that make many older children's books inappropriate for younger readers.

And of course, among children, there is the "fat book" phenomenon, in which children insist on checking out thick books beyond their understanding because they think it makes them look smart. If the "fat books" they've selected are not age appropriate, try to steer these children to the nonfiction collection where thick books are available, written to a younger understanding level. These nonfiction books include joke books, collections of fairy tales, short stories, poetry, and collective biographies. "Fat books" from the juvenile ghost and horror short story collections, frequently overlooked, work wonderfully with these children too.

Another way to direct children to age appropriate materials is by physical arrangement of the children's area. Place board books in wicker baskets on the floor to make them accessible to toddlers. Separate the Young Adult/Teen area from the Juvenile area by magazine shelves or display cases to help each group feel more comfortable.

Be proactive on suggesting age appropriate material, and be aware that inappropriate materials may have made their way into your collection. No matter how beautifully illustrated in picture book format, classic French short stories are not appropriate for seven-year-olds.

Internet

Children's librarians need to guide young people in Internet use. The Internet is a mixed blessing for libraries and children's librarians. While it provides access to a vast amount of information on every conceivable topic, the access is indiscriminate. Material not suitable for children (and information that is blatantly wrong) is mixed in with great sites for kids and cutting-edge data.

Your library should have an acceptable use policy that governs use of the Internet. This policy should apply equally to all Internet users, regardless of age. It should be supported by procedures that stipulate requirements for use (such as a valid library card), length of time allowed per session, appropriate uses, and the consequences of inappropriate use.

As with other library materials, parents alone have the right to decide what they want their children to read and view on a computer, and they can decide these issues only for their own children.

Whether or not your library's computers are filtered is another matter of Board policy. Since filters are not perfect, filtering is no guarantee that children will never have access to something inappropriate. In fact, some children perceive filtering as a challenge to overcome. Instituting filters also implies that children are protected from access to an inappropriate site—thus leaving the library open to a lawsuit if inappropriate information makes its way past the filter.

If your library is considering an acceptable use policy or is in the process of revising its policy, *Children and the Internet: Guidelines for Developing Public Library Policy* (ALA, 1998) will be helpful. This publication is a joint venture by the Association for Library Trustees and Advocates, the Association for Library Service to Children, and the Public Library Association (PLA). It offers acceptable use philosophy, examples of policies, and an essay by Will Manley on what he believes is a hypocritical anti-censorship stance.

Problem Behavior

All public libraries should have procedures to deal with unattended children as well as procedures for dealing with disruptive patrons in general. These procedures must be firmly based in library policy approved by the Board. They should be consistent with local and state laws; for example, a truancy law may preclude an unattended child's presence in the library during school hours without parental supervision.

In many cases, what is perceived as problem behavior by children in the library is actually the direct consequence of the behavior of the child's parent or caregiver. A four-year-old who wanders into your restricted work area is not being supervised by a parent, and the fourteen-year-old is waiting for a ride home after the library closes because her parents are late picking her up.

Be sure you know the library's policy and appropriate course of action or procedures that deal with unattended children. When you discuss it with staff, parents, and children, be sure to stress that these policies and procedures are to ensure children's safety. Specify the age children are allowed in the children's area without an adult or caretaker supervising them. Also state the minimum age for a caretaker (possibly the prevailing local babysitter minimum age), so that a seven-year-old big sister can't be the caretaker for twin three-year-olds sent to the children's area. Also spell out the procedure for the safety of children left after hours. Finally, include a statement to the effect that staff cannot supervise or babysit children; parents are responsible for their children's behavior.

As a librarian you may be required by law to report any suspected cases of abuse or abandonment. If your state has such laws, they may give you another solution to parents who leave their children for long periods unsupervised in the library.

A policy for disruptive patrons may distinguish between those over or under a certain age as to the number of warnings that will be given and who will receive the warnings. For example, the policy may specify that a child under eight who is disruptive will be asked to quiet down, then her parent will be asked to control her, and then the family will be asked to leave the library. It may also specify that a disruptive patron older than eight will be given only one warning.

Dealing with Difficult People in the Library by Mark Willis (ALA, 1999) covers these policies thoroughly, with examples. His chapter entitled, "Hey Lady! You Forgot Your Kids!" will be especially helpful.

Storytime behavior guidelines are a good teaching tool. They help both the children and their parents know what is expected of them. Storytime guidelines can cover age limits (children who are too old or too young for storytime are more likely to be disruptive, as they are likely bored). They can also make suggestions to parents for dealing with misbehaving or noisy children (and thereby subtly reinforce that parents do need to monitor their children). The guidelines can also give directional information ("If you arrive after storytime has started, please enter by the door behind the reference desk to minimize disruption."). Storytime behavior guidelines may also have to mention that parents should turn off their phones and pagers and not converse during the program.

Work with your library's administrators to make sure that sound policies are in place and that there are reasonable procedures to fairly implement these policies. Having solid policies and procedures will enable your library to strike a balance between being all-welcoming and ensuring the safety and comfort of everyone concerned.

11

Recordkeeping and Professional Development

Recordkeeping

Keeping good records and being able to report the numbers when requested are important for the children's department, your library, and the profession. Grant proposals also benefit from good records.

Use a phone diary and journal to assist you in documenting how much time you spend on the phone and how you manage your day. Information from these tools can be used to support the department's activities. They can also aid in prioritizing your work, especially if all you seem to accomplish is putting out fires.

As mentioned in the programming section, valid statistics can help you decide when to change a program or what program to change. Are you getting forty three-year-olds on Mondays but only twelve on Tuesdays? Has the Book Discussion Group's attendance really dropped off now that Soccer League has started? Did your summer reading program have twice as many children participate from the schools you visited to publicize it, compared to children from the schools where you only sent flyers about the program?

In your programming attendance statistics, include a column for counting the attendance at programs you presented away from the library. Too often these numbers are forgotten. In-library program attendance is typically counted by the program. Programs presented away from the library may be counted only by the number of library personnel who present them, not by how many programs were presented.

If you prepare a monthly report of activity for your supervisor or for inclusion in a report to the Board, remember to include items such as community contacts you have made. Also include professional development you have undertaken. If you participated in an online tutorial on copyright or a "meet the author chat," be sure to let your supervisor know.

Find out what statistics your state library requests from your director and how they are defined. These statistics reflect how your library ranks among other libraries serving similar populations. Start saving those numbers if you are not already.

Finally, take time to complete and return surveys and studies being done by other children's librarians and graduate students. The field suffers from a lack of serious scholarship and concrete data backing up what we know to be fact: children need libraries, and libraries change lives.

Keep a copy of these reports and statistics that you compile. They will become a record of your accomplishments and be useful for citing in your own professional advancement.

Career Opportunities

Children's librarianship has many opportunities. Children's librarianship skills are readily transportable around the country, and there are many types of employment opportunities available.

If you are working in children's services and don't yet have an advanced degree, a number of ALA scholarships are available for further education. The Mary V. Gaver Scholarship of $3,000 is awarded annually by ALA. Two ALSC scholarship programs are the Bound to Stay Bound Books Scholarship (three $6,000 annual awards) and the Frederic G. Melcher Scholarship (two $6,000 annual awards). The ALSC scholarships have a narrow window of application time, just the time between the applicant's acceptance to an accredited library school and before course work begins. Recipients of the ALSC scholarships agree to work in children's services for a year following graduation.

Participation in library professional organizations is helpful to your professional development. Join the American Library Association and the Association for Library Service to Children to connect with others who share your goals. These organizations also provide you with a network for support and information. You can even participate on ALSC committees electronically if you cannot get away regularly for conferences.

ALSC offers awards to attend conferences. These awards are made to children's librarians who have never attended conferences, or who have developed an outstanding reading or literature program. Penguin Putnam Books for Young Readers Awards for $600 each are awarded to enable four children's librarians who are ALSC members to attend ALA's Annual Conference. The ALSC/Econo-Clad Award honors an ALSC member who has developed an outstanding reading or literature program for children with $1000 to be spent attending ALA's Annual Conference.

Join your state or regional library association's children's section, as well. Participation on a state level is beneficial in many ways, not the least of which is knowing who to call with a state-related question.

Find out about distance learning opportunities offered at various colleges and universities, as well as by state libraries. Explore how these opportunities might relate to your professional development and interests, and take advantage of them.

Storyteller's groups, puppetry guilds, children's book review groups, and many other programming or library oriented groups will help you network and learn. Internet discussion groups are another way to connect with others interested in children's books and children's services. Technology may not have changed the essence of children's services, but it has made working in the field less isolated.

Professional Resources

Organizations

American Library Association
50 E. Huron St.
Chicago, IL 60611-2795
www.ala.org

Association for Library Service to
   Children
50 E. Huron St.
Chicago, IL 60611-2795
www.ala.org/alsc

Professional Publications

American Libraries
   Monthly journal of the American Library Association

*Book Links: Connecting Books,
Libraries, and Classrooms*
   Published bimonthly by ALA for teachers, librarians, and parents

Booklist
Published biweekly by ALA; reviews of books and electronic media

The Bulletin of the Center for Children's Books
Published monthly by the University of Illinois; articles and reviews

The Horn Book Guide to Children's and Young Adult Books
Published semiannually by The Horn Book; collected reviews from *The Horn Book Magazine*

The Horn Book Magazine
Published bimonthly by The Horn Book; articles and reviews

Journal of Youth Services in Libraries/JOYS
Quarterly journal of ALSC and YALSA

Kirkus Reviews
Published biweekly by Kirkus Associates; reviews

School Library Journal
Published monthly by Reed Elsevier; articles and reviews

VOYA: Voice of Youth Advocates
Published bimonthly by Scarecrow; articles and reviews

Resources

Die cut shape sources for name tags, crafts and bulletin boards

Accu-Cut
1035 E. Dodge
P.O. Box 1053
Fremont, NE 68025
Phone: (800) 253-2238
Fax: (800) 253-2240
info@accucut.com
http://www.accucut.com

Ellison Educational
Equipment, Inc.
25862 Commercentre Dr.
Lake Forest, CA 92630-8804
Phone: (800) 288-1670
Fax: (800) 369-1332
info@ellison.com
http://www.ellison.com

Conclusion

12

Many aspects of librarianship in general have changed over the last two decades with the advent of personal computers and the Internet. The essence of children's librarianship, however, has stayed much the same. We focus on providing books, information, and reading guidance to children. We are advocates for children within the library, the community, and the nation.

Children's librarians do indeed influence young lives by connecting the right child with the right book at the right time and by standing up for that child's right to read that book. Technology has changed some of the ways we find and distribute information, but it has yet to progress to the point of being able to lead small children in the chicken dance, to enthrall an audience with a story, or to judge a pet show.

While this book does not cover all aspects of children's librarianship, I have tried to include the information necessary that someone who may not be trained as a children's librarian needs to be able to do her job successfully.

Top Ten Ways to Be a Better Children's Librarian

1. Talk to children of all ages. Find out what's important to them, including TV shows, video games, books, hobbies, and other interests. Let children and their parents know you are sincerely interested in them.

2. READ, READ, READ children's books. Become familiar with the series that children want to read. Be able to recommend good children's books. Know something about books they may need to read for a state award or class assignment. Become familiar with such Web sites as the New York Public Library's list of one hundred picture books everyone should read (http://www.nypl.org/branch/kids/gloria.html).

3. Keep up with what is going on in the library world. Read news articles. Follow the debates affecting children's library services, such as challenges to materials like the Harry Potter books and the use of filters for library Internet access.

4. Observe others doing storytime. Visit programs at other libraries, bookstores, schools, and so on.

5. Network at every opportunity. Get to know local librarians and arrange meetings between school and public librarians. Join state, regional, and national associations, like ALSC. Join electronic discussion lists like ALSC-L.

6. Read publications to help you, such as *Journal of Youth Services in Libraries* and *Book Links*. Subscribe to them or borrow them from another library.

7. Keep up your computer skills, and use software used by young people. Become an expert in helping children find the information they need for homework assignments and hobbies.

8. Be an innovator. Try new activities, events, and projects like "Blow Up the Librarian" Science Day, or a storytime holiday parade through a nearby nursing home. Let children and their parents know that libraries are exciting and welcoming places.

9. Never stop learning. Take a storytelling class or workshop. Attend a preconference or leadership seminar. Go to professional conferences to learn more about your craft.

10. Be able to articulate clearly why you believe children's library services are important, and be ready to speak up for them at every opportunity.

SOURCE: Adapted from *Loose Change*, The Newsletter of the Northeast Kansas Library System, Dec. 1999, Vol. 4, Issue 12

Competencies for Librarians Serving Children in Public Libraries REVISED EDITION

Association for Library Service to Children, a division of the American Library Association

A

Effective library service for children entails a broad range of experience and professional skills. The librarian serving children is first of all fully knowledgeable in the theories, practices and emerging trends of librarianship but must also have specialized knowledge of the particular needs of child library users.

In developing both the original and this revised document, the committees preparing the Competencies looked at numerous sets of standards for children's services from state agencies, professional associations and individual libraries and systems. These competencies are broadly categorized into the following areas: knowledge of the client group; administrative and managerial skills; communications skills; materials and collection development; programming skills; advocacy, public relations and networking; and professionalism and professional development.

Although the *Competencies* seek to define the role of the librarian serving children, they will apply in varying degrees according to the professional responsibilities of each individual job situation. The assignment of responsibilities for planning, managing and delivering library services to children will vary in relation to the size and staffing pattern of the local public library. It is recognized that not all children's librarians in all positions will be involved in all of these activities, nor will they need all of these skills. Some libraries will have only one librarian responsible for providing all service to children, others will have more than one professional children's librarian sharing those responsibilities. In larger libraries with multiple outlets, there may be a coordinator or manager of children's services who oversees the planning, training, design and delivery of service by a number of building level service providers. Because the variety of situations and responsibilities differ so widely, these *Competencies* seek to be all-inclusive rather than to categorize minimum levels of activities and skills needed to serve children in the public library.

The philosophical underpinning for children's services in all public libraries is that children are entitled to full access to the full range of library materials and services available to any other library customer. Other documents that affirm this service philosophy include the American Library Association's (ALA) Library Bill of Rights, the Freedom to Read and Freedom to View statements of ALA.

It is the policy of this organization that a master's degree from a library/information program from an ALA accredited graduate school is the appropriate professional degree for the librarian serving children in the public library.

The following *Competencies* make it clear that the children's librarian must do more than simply provide age-appropriate service. Children's librarians must also be advocates for their clientele both within the library and in the larger society, and they must also demonstrate the full range of professional and managerial skills demanded of any other librarians.

Each edition of the *Competencies* has been arranged in a systematic manner beginning with knowledge of the community and client group. This gives a solid foundation for planning and managing. Communication is always a vital skill to articulate goals and objectives. Collection development provides the resources for services and programs. Finally, the future of service to children depends on advocacy and professional development. As society changes, so does the public library, and so must the public librarian. Professional growth and development is a career-long process.

It is recommended that libraries developing their own competencies or standards for service to children use this document in conjunction with relevant state standards or guidelines.

I. Knowledge of Client Group

    1. Understands theories of infant, child, and adolescent learning and development and their implications for library service.

    2 Recognizes the effects of societal developments on the needs of children.

    3. Assesses the community regularly and systematically to identify community needs, tastes, and resources.

4. Identifies clients with special needs as a basis for designing and implementing services, following Americans with Disabilities Act (ADA) and state and local regulations where appropriate.

5. Recognizes the needs of an ethnically diverse community.

6. Understands and responds to the needs of parents, care givers, and other adults who use the resources of the children's department.

7. Creates an environment in the children's area, which provides for enjoyable and convenient use of library resources.

8. Maintains regular communication with other agencies, institutions, and organizations serving children in the community.

II. Administrative and Management Skills

1. Participates in all aspects of the library's planning process to represent and support children's services.

2. Sets long and short-range goals, objectives, and priorities.

3. Analyzes the costs of library services to children in order to develop, justify, administer/manage, and evaluate a budget.

4. Writes job descriptions and interviews, trains, encourages continuing education, and evaluates staff who work with children, consulting with other library administrations as indicated in library personnel policy.

5. Demonstrates problem-solving, decision making, and mediation techniques.

6. Delegates responsibility appropriately and supervises staff constructively.

7. Documents and evaluates services.

8. Identifies outside sources of funding and writes effective grant applications.

9. Applies appropriate tools to implement and facilitate management functions.

III. Communication Skills

1. Defines and communicates the needs of children so that administrators, other library staff, and members of the larger community understand the basis for children's services.

2. Demonstrates interpersonal skills in meeting with children, parents, staff, and community.

3. Adjusts to the varying demands of writing planning documents, procedures, guidelines, press releases, memoranda, reports, grant applications, annotations, and reviews in all formats, including print and electronic.

4. Speaks effectively when addressing individuals, as well as small and large groups.

5. Applies active listening skills.

6. Conducts productive formal and informal reference interviews.

7. Communicates constructively with "problem patrons."

IV. Materials and Collection Development

   A. Knowledge of Materials

      1. Demonstrates a knowledge and appreciation of children's literature, periodicals, audiovisual materials, Websites and other electronic media, and other materials that constitute a diverse, current, and relevant children's collection.

      2. Keeps abreast of new materials and those for retrospective purchase by consulting a wide variety of reviewing sources and publishers' catalogs, including those of small presses; by attending professional meetings; and by reading, viewing, and listening.

      3. Is aware of adult reference materials and other library resources, which may serve the needs of children and their caregivers.

   B. Ability to Select Appropriate Materials and Develop a Children's Collection

      1. Evaluates and recommends collection development, selection and weeding policies for children's materials consistent with the mission and policies of the parent library and the ALA Library Bill of Rights, and applies these policies in acquiring and weeding materials for or management of the children's collection.

2. Acquires materials that reflect the ethnic diversity of the community, as well as the need of children to become familiar with other ethnic groups and cultures.

3. Understands and applies criteria for evaluating the content and artistic merit of children's materials in all genres and formats.

4. Keeps abreast of current issues in children's materials collections and formulates a professional philosophy with regard to these issues.

5. Demonstrates a knowledge of technical services, cataloging and indexing procedures, and practices relating to children's materials.

C. Ability to Provide Customers with Appropriate Materials and Information

1. Connects children to the wealth of library resources, enabling them to use libraries effectively.

2. Matches children and their families with materials appropriate to their interest and abilities.

3. Provides help where needed, respects children's right to browse, and answers questions regardless of their nature or purpose.

4. Assists and instructs children in information gathering and research skills as appropriate.

5. Understands and applies search strategies to give children full and equitable access to information from the widest possible range of sources, such as children's and adult reference works, indexes, catalogs, electronic resources, information and referral files, and interlibrary loan networks.

6. Compiles and maintains information about community resources so that children and adults working with children can be referred to appropriate sources of assistance.

7. Works with library technical services to guarantee that the children's collection is organized and accessed for the easiest possible use.

8. Creates bibliographies, booktalks, displays, electronic documents, and other special tools to increase access to library resources and motivate their use.

V. Programming Skills

   1. Designs, promotes, executes, and evaluates programs for children
      of all ages, based on their developmental needs and interests and
      the goals of the library.

   2. Presents a variety of programs or brings in skilled resource people
      to present these programs, including storytelling, booktalking,
      book discussions, puppet programs, and other appropriate activi-
      ties.

   3. Provides outreach programs commensurate with community needs
      and library goals and objectives.

   4. Establishes programs and services for parents, individuals and
      agencies providing child-care, and other professionals in the com-
      munity who work with children.

VI. Advocacy, Public Relations, and Networking Skills

   1. Promotes an awareness of and support for meeting children's
      library and information needs through all media.

   2. Considers the opinions and requests of children in the develop-
      ment and evaluation of library services.

   3. Ensures that children have full access to library materials,
      resources, and services as prescribed by the Library Bill of
      Rights.

   4. Acts as liaison with other agencies in the community serving chil-
      dren, including other libraries and library systems.

   5. Develops cooperative programs between the public library,
      schools, and other community agencies.

   6. Extends library services to children and groups of children
      presently unserved.

   7. Utilizes effective public relations techniques and media to publi-
      cize library activities.

   8. Develops policies and procedures applying to children's services
      based on federal, state, and local law where appropriate.

   9. Understands library governance and the political process and lob-
      bies on behalf of children's services.

VII. Professionalism and Professional Development

1. Acknowledges the legacy of children's librarianship, its place in the context of librarianship as a whole, and past contributions to the profession.

2. Keeps abreast of current trends and emerging technologies, issues, and research in librarianship, child development, education, and allied fields.

3. Practices self-evaluation.

4. Conveys a nonjudgmental attitude toward patrons and their requests.

5. Demonstrates an understanding of and respect for diversity in cultural and ethnic values.

6. Knows and practices the American Library Association's Code of Ethics.

7. Preserves confidentiality in interchanges with patrons.

8. Works with library educators to meet needs of library school students and promote professional association scholarships.

9. Participates in professional organizations to strengthen skills, interact with fellow professionals, and contribute to the profession.

10. Understands that professional development and continuing education are activities to be pursued throughout one's career.

Approved by the Board of Directors of the Association for Library Service to Children, a division of the American Library Association, on June 26, 1999. Copies available for $3.00 from ALSC/ALA, 50 E. Huron St., Chicago, IL 60611. Copyright 1999 by ALSC.

B Statement of Commitment to Excellence in Library Service to Children in a Technological Age

Technology, specifically the Internet, is revolutionizing how we live, learn and work. No other technology in history has provided us with so much information so easily. Recognizing that the Internet has raised concerns about children's access to potentially harmful material, the Association for Library Service to Children affirms the commitment of children's librarians across America to ensuring a positive library experience for children.

We are committed to:

Providing collections, services and assistance that encourage and support children in exploring the world of ideas and information and in developing the knowledge and skills they need to live, learn, work and govern in a democratic society;

Selecting and guiding children to age appropriate materials in print, video and online;

Providing instruction for children and parents about online searches and other techniques to ensure a positive Internet experience;

Respecting the right of parents to decide which materials are appropriate for their children;

Advising children and parents on the selection of materials they read and view and to make positive choices;

Developing policies and services that recognize and serve the wide ranging needs of children that include, but are not limited to, differences in their emotional and intellectual maturity and family values;

Educating parents about the Internet and encouraging them to take an active role in guiding their children's use;

Compiling and recommending quality Web sites for children; and

Taking an active role in developing Internet policies and programs that help parents protect their children from inappropriate material and ensure children's access to information they need.

This commitment is expressed daily in communities across America. We encourage everyone to visit their local library to learn more about this important and valuable new resource and about the policies and programs in place to provide a positive and enriching experience for children.

Approved by the ALSC Board of Directors at the Midwinter Meeting in San Antonio, January 14-19, 2000.

C

Bibliographies of Children's Books

The following bibliographies include books that have been discussed in the text and other books for young people.

Great American Biographies for Young People

Younger Grades (K-3)

Adler, David
Picture Book of Amelia Earhart
Holiday, 1998

Brenner, Barbara
The Boy Who Loved to Draw:
    Benjamin West
Houghton, 1999

Brown, Don
Alice Ramsey's Grand Adventure
Houghton, 1997

Bruchac, Joseph
A Boy Called Slow: The True Story
    of Sitting Bull
Philomel, 1995

Bunting, Eve
Once upon a Time
Owen, 1995

Carlson, Laurie
Boss of the Plains: The Hat That
    Won the West
DK Publishing, 1998

Coles, Robert
Story of Ruby Bridges
Scholastic, 1995

Cooney, Barbara
Eleanor
Viking, 1996

DePaola, Tomie
26 Fairmont Street
Putnam, 1999

Ehlert, Lois
Under My Nose
Owen, 1996

Heller, Ruth
Fine Lines
Owen, 1996

Hodges, Margaret
True Tale of Johnny Appleseed
Holiday, 1997

Krull, Kathleen
Wilma Unlimited: How Wilma Rudolph Became the World's Fastest Woman
Harcourt, 1996

Lied, Kate
Potato: A Story of the Great Depression
National, 1997

Lyon, George Ella
A Wordful Child
Owen, 1996

Martin, Jacqueline
Snowflake Bentley
Houghton, 1998

McGill, Alice
Molly Bannaky
Houghton, 1999

Miller, William
Frederick Douglass: The Last Day of Slavery
Lee, 1995

Pinkney, Andrea
Bill Pickett: Rodeo-Ridin' Cowboy
Gulliver, 1996

San Souci, Robert
Kate Shelley: Bound for Legend
Dial, 1995

Schroeder, Alan
Minty: The Story of the Young Harriet Tubman
Dial, 1996

Stevenson, James
I Had a Lot of Wishes
Greenwillow, 1995

Wallner, Alexandra
Laura Ingalls Wilder
Holiday, 1997

Whiteley, Opal
Only Opal: The Diary of a Young Girl
Philomel, 1994

Younger, Barbara
Purple Mountain Majesties: Story of Katherine Lee Bates and America the Beautiful
Dutton, 1998

Older Grades (4-6)

Ada, Alma Flor
Under the Royal Palms
Atheneum, 1998

Bauer, Marion
Writer's Story from Life to Fiction
Clarion, 1995

Bridges, Ruby
Through My Eyes
Scholastic, 1999

Cole, Joanna; Saul, Wendy
On the Bus with Joanna Cole
Heinemann, 1996

Coleman, Evelyn
Riches of Osceola McCarty
Whitman, 1998

Ellsworth, Mary Ellen
*Gertrude Chandler Warner and the
    Boxcar Children*
Whitman, 1997

Engel, Dean; Freedman, Florence
*Ezra Jack Keats: A Biography with
    Illustrations*
Silver Moon, 1995

Fleischman, Sid
Abracadabra Kid: A Writer's Life
Greenwillow, 1996

Freedman, Russell
Life and Death of Crazy Horse
Holiday, 1996

Fritz, Jean
*Harriet Beecher Stowe and the
    Beecher Preachers*
Putnam, 1994

Fritz, Jean
Homesick: My Own Story
Putnam, 1982

Fritz, Jean
*You Want Women to Vote, Lizzie
    Stanton?*
Putnam, 1995

Giblin, James
*Charles A. Lindbergh: A Human
    Hero*
Clarion, 1997

Kehret, Peg
Small Steps: The Year I Got Polio
Whitman, 1996

Krull, Katherine
*Lives of the Presidents: Fame,
    Shame (and What the Neighbors
    Thought)*
Harcourt, 1998

Lasky, Kathryn
*Brilliant Streak: The Making of
    Mark Twain*
Harcourt, 1998

Lowry, Lois
Looking Back: A Book of Memories
Houghton, 1998

Matthews, Tom
*Always Inventing: A
    Photobiography of Alexander
    Graham Bell*
National Geographic Society, 1999

McCurdy, Michael (ed.)
*Escape from Slavery: The Boyhood
    of Frederick Douglass in His
    Own Words*
Knopf, 1994

McPhail, David
In Flight with David McPhail
Heinemann, 1996

O'Grady, Scott; French, Michael
*Basher Five-Two: The True Story of
    F-16 Fighter Pilot Captain
    Scott O'Grady*
Doubleday, 1997

Peet, Bill
Bill Peet: An Autobiography
Houghton, 1989

Reef, Catherine
Walt Whitman
Clarion, 1995

Rice, Dorothy; Walthall, Lucille
Seventeenth Child
Linnet, 1998

Spinelli, Jerry
Knots in My Yo-Yo String: The Autobiography of a Kid
Knopf, 1998

Stanley, Jerry
Frontier Merchants: Lionel and Barron Jacobs and the Jewish Pioneers Who Settled the West
Crown, 1998

Stine, R. L.; Arthur, Joe
It Came from Ohio!
Scholastic, 1997

Szabo, Corine
Sky Pioneer: A Photobiography of Amelia Earhart
National, 1997

Thompson, Peggy
Katie Henio, Navajo Sheepherder
Cobblehill, 1995

Wadsworth, Ginger
John Burroughs: The Sage of Slabsides
Clarion, 1997

Favorite Books for Storytime, Storytelling, and Booktalking

Allard, Harry; Marshall, James (illus.)
Miss Nelson Is Missing!
Houghton Mifflin, 1977

Aylesworth, Jim; Christelow, Eileen (illus.)
Complete Hickory Dickory Dock
Atheneum, 1990

Aylesworth, Jim; Gammell, Stephen (illus.)
Old Black Fly
Holt, 1992

Bang, Molly
Ten, Nine, Eight
Greenwillow, 1983

Barton, Byron
Trucks
Crowell, 1986

Bradman, Tony; Chamberlain, Margaret
Look Out, He's behind You!
Putnam, 1988

Brown, Margaret Wise; Hurd, Clement (illus.)
Goodnight, Moon
Harper, 1947

Burton, Virginia
Mike Mulligan and His Steam Shovel
Houghton, 1939

Carle, Eric
The Very Busy Spider
Philomel, 1984

Carle, Eric
The Very Quiet Cricket
Philomel, 1990

Cleary, Beverly
Strider
Morrow, 1991

Cole, Joanna; Calmenson,
   Stephanie; Tiegreen, Alan (illus.)
Six Sick Sheep
Morrow, 1993

Crews, Donald
Freight Train
Morrow, 1978

Dalokay, Vedat
Sister Shako and Kolo the Goat
Lothrop, 1994

DePaola, Tomie
Charlie Needs a Cloak
Prentice-Hall, 1974

De Regniers, Beatrice; Montresor,
   Beni (illus.)
May I Bring a Friend?
Atheneum, 1965

Erickson, John
*Original Adventures of Hank the
   Cowdog*
Maverick, 1983

Flack, Marjorie; Wiese, Kurt (illus.)
Story about Ping
Viking, 1933

Fleming, Denise
In the Tall, Tall Grass
Holt, 1991

Fleming, Denise
Lunch
Holt, 1992

Fleischman, Sid
Whipping Boy
Greenwillow, 1986

Florian, Douglas
People Working
Crowell, 1983

Freeman, Don
Corduroy
Viking, 1968

Gag, Wanda
Millions of Cats
Coward-McCane, 1928

Gibson, Fred
Old Yeller
Harper, 1956

Ginsburg, Mirra; Aruego, Jose
   (illus.); Dewey, Ariane (illus.)
Mushroom in the
Macmillan, 1974

Gretz, Susanna; Sage, Alison
Teddy Bears Cure a Cold
Macmillan, 1984

Hall, Donald; Cooney, Barbara
   (illus.)
Ox-Cart Man
Viking, 1979

Henkes, Kevin
Lilly's Purple Plastic Purse
Greenwillow, 1996

Hoban, Tana
26 Letters and 99 Cents
Greenwillow, 1987

Hoban, Tana
Round & Round & Round
Greenwillow, 1983

Hogrogian, Nonny
One Fine Day
Macmillian, 1971

Hutchins, Pat
The Doorbell Rang
Greenwillow, 1986

Hutchins, Pat
Good-Night Owl!
Collier, 1972

Jonas, Ann
Round Trip
Greenwillow, 1983

Kasza, Keiko
A Mother for Choco
Putnam, 1992

Keats, Ezra
The Snowy Day
Viking, 1962

Kent, Jack
Fat Cat
Parent's Magazine Press, 1971

Kent, Jack
Little Peep
Prentice Hall, 1981

Kent, Jack
Round Robin
Prentice-Hall, 1982

Kovalski, Maryann
The Wheels on the Bus
Little, 1987

Krasilovsky, Phyllis
Man Who Didn't Wash His Dishes
Doubleday, 1950

Kraus, Robert; Aruego, Jose (illus.)
Leo the Late Bloomer
Crowell, 1971

Lester, Julius; Pinto, Ralph (illus.)
*The Knee-High Man and Other
    Tales (Why Dogs Hate Cats)*
Dial, 1972

Llewellyn, Claire
Mighty Machines: Truck
DK Publishing, 1995

MacLachlan, Patricia
Sarah, Plain and Tall
Harper, 1985

Mann, Pamela; Newton, Jill
    (illus.)
Frog Princess
Gareth Stevens, 1995

Marshall, James
The Three Pigs
Dial, 1989

Martin, Bill; Archambault, John;/
    Ehlert, Lois (illus.)
Chicka Chicka Boom Boom
Simon & Schuster, 1989

McCloskey, Robert
Make Way for Ducklings
Viking, 1941

McKissack, Patricia
The Dark-Thirty
Knopf, 1992

McKissack, Patricia; Isadora,
    Rachel (illus.)
Flossie and The Fox
Dial, 1986

Mitchell, Margaree; Ransome,
    James (illus.)
Uncle Jed's Barbershop
Simon & Schuster, 1993

Moore, Clement; Marshall, James
    (illus.)
The Night before Christmas
Scholastic, 1985

Mosel, Arlene; Lent, Blair (illus.)
The Funny Little Woman
Dutton, 1972

Murphy, Jill
Five Minutes Peace
Putnam, 1986

Keats, Ezra Jack (illus.)
Over in the Meadow
Four Winds, 1971

Paul, Ann; Graham, Mark (illus.)
Shadows Are About
Scholastic, 1992

Payne, Emmy; Rey, H.A. (illus.)
Katy No-Pocket
Houghton Mifflin, 1944

Pickett, Anola; Delaney, Ned (illus.)
Old Enough for Magic
Harper, 1989

Pomerantz, Charlotte; Aruego, Jose
    (illus.); Dewey, Ariane (illus.)
One Duck, Another Duck
Greenwillow, 1984

Prelutsky, Jack; Stevenson, James
    (illus.)
New Kid on the Block
Greenwillow, 1984

Prelutsky, Jack; Stevenson, James
    (illus.)
Something Big Has Been Here
Scholastic, 1992

Provensen, Alice; Provensen,
    Martin
*The Glorious Flight: Across the
    Channel with Louis Bleriot*
Viking, 1983

Quackenbush, Robert
Skip to My Lou
Lippincott, 1975

Rathmann, Peggy
Officer Buckle And Gloria
Putnam, 1995

Rounds, Glen
*Three Little Pigs and the Big,
    Bad Wolf*
Holiday House, 1992

Rynbach, Iris
Five Little Pumpkins
Boyds Mill, 1995

Scieszka, Jon; Smith, Lane (illus.)
True Story of the Three Little Pigs
Viking, 1989

Sendak, Maurice
Where the Wild Things Are
Harper, 1963

Seuss, Dr.
Green Eggs and Ham
Random, 1968

Shannon, David
No, David!
Blue Sky, 1998

Sharmat, Mitchell; Aruego, Jose
    (illus.); Dewey, Ariane (illus.)
Gregory the Terrible Eater
Four Winds, 1980

Shaw, Nancy
Sheep in a Jeep
Houghton, 1986

Slobodkina, Esphyr
Caps for Sale
W.R. Scott, 1947

Soto, Gary; Martinez, Ed (illus.)
Too Many Tamales
Putnam, 1993

Spier, Peter (illus.)
Erie Canal
Doubleday, 1970

Steig, William
Pete's a Pizza
HarperCollins, 1998

Steig, William
Sylvester and the Magic Pebble
Windmill, 1969

Stevens, Janet
Tops and Bottoms
Harcourt, 1995

Swartz, Alvin; Zimmer, Dirk (illus.)
*In a Dark, Dark Room and Other
    Scary Stories*
HarperCollins, 1984

Taback, Sims
*There Was an Old Lady Who
    Swallowed a Fly*
Viking, 1997

Titherington, Jeanne
Pumpkin, Pumpkin
Greenwillow, 1986

Trivizas, Eugene; Oxenbury, Helen
    (illus.)
*Three Little Wolves and the Big
    Bad Pig*
Macmillan, 1993

Tudor, Tasha
A Is for Annabelle
Walck, 1954

Viorst, Judith; Cruz, Ray (illus.)
*Alexander and the Terrible,
    Horrible, No Good Very Bad Day*
Atheneum, 1972

Waddell, Martin; Oxenbury, Helen
    (illus.)
Farmer Duck
Candlewick, 1991

Wells, Rosemary
McDuff and the Baby
Hyperion, 1997

Wells, Rosemary
Peabody
Dial, 1983

White, E.B.
Charlotte's Web
Harper, 1952

Wood, Audrey; Wood, Don (illus.)
*The Napping House Wakes Up (A
   Mechanical Book)*
Harcourt, 1994

Wood, Audrey
Silly Sally
Harcourt, 1992

Yolen, Jane; Schoenherr, John
   (illus.)
Owl Moon
Philomel, 1987

Young, Ed
Seven Blind Mice
Putnam, 1992

Zemach, Harve; Zemach, Margot
   (illus.)
Judge
Farrar, 1969

Professional Publications

Programming Resources

Allison, Christine
I'll Tell You a Story, I'll Sing You a Song
Delacorte, 1987
> Very useful compilation of storylines, poems, fables, etc., with extra information on presentation.

ALSC Preschool Services Committee
First Steps to Literacy
ALSC, 1990
> Library programs for parents, teachers, and caregivers.

Anderson, Dee
Amazingly Easy Puppet Plays
ALA, 1997
> Forty-two new scripts for one-person puppet shows.

Baltuck, Naomi
Crazy Gibberish and Other Story Hour Stretches
Linnet, 1993

Bannister, Mary
Storybook Connections: Fairy Tale Activities from A to Z
Monday Morning, 1995
> Arts, crafts, dramatic play, literature links, etc. for pre-K–1.

Bauer, Caroline Feller
Celebrations: Read-Aloud Holiday and Theme Book Programs
Wilson, 1985
> Complete program with bulletin boards, texts, bibliography, etc.

Bauer, Caroline Feller
Leading Kids to Books through Magic
ALA, 1996
> Mighty Easy Motivators series.

Bauer, Caroline Feller
Leading Kids to Books through Puppets
ALA, 1997
> Mighty Easy Motivators series.

Bauer, Caroline Feller
New Handbook for Storytellers
ALA, 1994
> Ultimate resource for storytelling. Includes props, flannel boards, puppets, and good story suggestions.

Bauer, Caroline Feller
This Way to Books
Wilson, 1983
> Programs, costumes, bookmarks, booktalks, poetry, lots and lots of ideas on ways to bring kids and books together.

Briggs, Diane
101 Fingerplays, Stories, and Songs to Use with Finger Puppets
ALA, 1999

Carlson, Ann D.
Flannelboard Stories for Infants and Toddlers
ALA, 1999

Colgin, Mary Lou (compiler)
One Potato, Two Potato, Three Potato, Four: 165 Chants for Children
Gryphon House, 1996
> Chants grouped by subject includes those about food, seasons, people, etc.

Cook, Sybilla Avery; Page, Cheryl A.
Books, Battles, and Bees
ALA, 1994
> A reader's competition resource for intermediate grades.

Cromwell, Liz; Hibner, Dixie; Faitel, John
Finger Frolics: Finger plays for Young Children
Gryphon House, 1983
> Old and new finger plays, activity verses, etc., grouped by subject.

Cullum, Carolyn
Storytime Source Book
Neal-Schuman, 1990
> 100 storytimes with filmstrips, films, books, finger plays, crafts and activities all lined out for you.

De Wit, Dorothy
Children's Faces Looking Up: Program Building for the Storyteller
ALA, 1979
> Approachable suggestions and six complete storytimes from a master storyteller.

DeSpain, Pleasant
Thirty-Three Multicultural Tales to Tell
August House, 1993
> Country of origin given as well as motifs traced.

DeSpain, Pleasant
Twenty-two Splendid Tales to Tell, 3rd ed.
August House, 1994
> International folktales with clever hooks for fun telling.

Dowell, Ruth
Move Over, Mother Goose! Finger plays, Action Verses, and Funny Rhymes
Gryphon House, 1987
 A new collection of fingerplays, grouped by subject.

Ernst, Linda L.
Lapsit Services for the Very Young
Neal-Schuman, 1995
 How-to manual.

Jeffery, Debby Ann
Literate Beginnings
ALA, 1995
 Programs for babies and toddlers.

Kladder, Jeri
Story Hour
McFarland, 1995
 55 preschool programs for public libraries.

Kobrin, Beverly
Eyeopeners
Penguin, 1988
 How to choose and use children's books about real people, places, and things.

Kobrin, Beverly
Eyeopeners II
Penguin, 1995
 More *Eyeopeners.*

Livo, Norma J. (ed. and retold)
Troubadour's Storybag
Fulcrum, 1996
 Musical folktales of the world.

MacDonald, Margaret Read
Booksharing: 101 Programs to Use with Preschoolers
Library Professional Publications, 1988
 Completely thought-out programs with book titles, songs, activities, and follow up activities.

MacDonald, Margaret Read
Parents Guide to Storytelling
HarperCollins, 1995
 How to make up new stories and retell old favorites.

MacDonald, Margaret Read
Peace Tales: World Folktales to Talk About
Linnet, 1992
 A collection of tales, fables, poems etc. under various headings to facilitate discussion and understanding.

MacDonald, Margaret Read
Storyteller's Start-Up Book: Finding, Learning, Performing, and Using Folktales
August House, 1993

Miller, Teresa (compiler)
Joining In
Yellow Moon, 1996
 An anthology of audience participation stories and how to tell them.

Milord, Susan
Hands around the World
Gareth Stevens, 1999

365 creative ways to build cultural awareness and global respect.

Milord, Susan
Tales Alive
Williamson, 1995
Ten multicultural folktales with activities.

Minkel, Walter
How to Do "Three Bears" with Two Hands
ALA, 2000
Performing with puppets.

Nelson, Esther
Silly Songbook
Sterling, 1981
Fun songs for kids.

Nespeca, Sue McCleaf
Library Programming for Families with Young Children
Neal-Schuman, 1994
How-to manual with samples.

Nichols, Judy
Storytimes for Two-Year-Olds, 2nd ed.
ALA, 1998
Background, how-to's, and suggested storytimes (with all their parts) for the two-year-old set.

Painter, William M.
Story Hours with Puppets and Other Props
Library Professional Publications, 1990
Ideas on how to enhance storytelling with the use of puppets.

Pellowski, Anne
Family Storytelling Handbook
Macmillan, 1987
How to use stories, anecdotes, rhymes, handkerchiefs, paper, and other objects to enrich your family traditions.

Press, Judy
Little Hands, Big Fun Craft Book
Williamson, 1996
Creative fun for two- to six-year-olds.

Reid, Rob
Family Storytimes
ALA, 1999
Twenty-four creative programs for all ages.

Schiller, Pam; Moore, Thomas
Where Is Thumbkin?
Gryphon House, 1993
500 activities to use with songs you already know.

Schimmel, Nancy
Just Enough to Tell a Story
Sisters Choice Press, 1992

Sierra, Judy
The Flannelboard Storytelling Book
H. W. Wilson, 1987
Thirty-six stories, poems and songs with patterns to use with the flannel board.

Sierra, Judy
Mother Goose's Playhouse
Bob Kammski Media, 1994
Toddler tales and nursery rhymes with patterns.

Sierra, Judy; Kaminski, Robert
*Multicultural Folktales: Stories to
Tell Young Children*
Oryx, 1991
Flannelboard stories sorted by
audience age and country.

Sitarz, Paula Gaj
*More Picture Book Story Hours:
From Parties to Pets*
Libraries Unlimited, 1990
Completely worked out story-
times with books, activities,
fingerplays and book talks.
Over twenty programs per
book.

Sitarz, Paula Gaj
*Picture Book Story Hours: From
Birthdays to Bears*
Libraries Unlimited, 1987
Completely worked out story-
times with books, activities,
fingerplays, etc.

Steven, Herb
*Using Children's Books in
Preschool Settings*
Neal-Schuman, 1994
A how-to manual.

Tashijian, Virginia
Juba This and Juba That, 2nd ed.
Little, 1995
Poems, stories and participa-
tion activities for storytime.

Tashijian, Virginia
With a Deep Sea Smile
Little, 1974
More storytime stretches.

Totline Staff; Mohrmann, Gary
(illus.)
*1001 Rhymes and Fingerplays for
Working with Young Children*
Warren, 1994

Works, Robin
*Promoting Reading with Reading
Programs*
Neal-Schuman Publishers, Inc.,
1987
A how-to manual.

Storytime Periodical Resources

Building Blocks
38W567 Brindlewood
Elgin, IL 60123
Activities, games, and art
activities for young children.

Copycat
P. O. Box 081546
Racine, WI 53408-1546

Mailbox
P.O. Box 51676
Boulder, CO 80323-1676
Offers 4 grade specific versions
with theme units, art activities,
bulletin board suggestions, etc.

Totline
P. O. Box 2255
Everett, WA 98203
Newsletter about young chil-
dren with storytime ideas,
snacks, parent flyers, etc.

Selection and Services Resources

ALA's Guide to Best Reading
ALA, annual

Allison, Christine
I'll Tell You a Story, I'll Sing You a Song
Delacorte, 1987
    Very useful compilation of storylines, poems, fables, etc., with extra information on presentation.

American Association of School Librarians
Information Literacy Standards for Student Learning
ALA, 1998

Barstow, Barbara
Beyond Picture Books, 2nd ed.
Bowker, 1995
    A guide to first readers.

Bodart-Talbot, Joni (ed.)
Booktalk!
Wilson, 1980
    Five volumes of booktalks and how-to information.

Borders, Sarah; Naylor, Alice Phoebe
Children Talking about Books
Oryx, 1993
    A guide to leading children's book discussions.

Children's Catalog, 17th ed.
Wilson, 1996

Colborn, Candy
What Do Children Read Next? A Reader's Guide to Fiction for Children, Volumes 1, 2
Gale, 1994

Connor, Jane Gardner
Children's Library Services Handbook
Oryx, 1990

Dreyer, Sharon
The Best of Bookfinder
American Guidance Service, 1992
    A guide to children's literature about interests and concerns of youth aged two through fifteen.

East, Kathy
Inviting Children's Authors and Illustrators
Neal-Schuman, 1995
    A how-to manual for school and public libraries, full of examples.

Elementary School Library Collection
Brodart, Revised biennially
    A guide to books and other media.

Eisenhut, Lynn (compiler)
Children's Services Training Manual
North State Cooperative Library System, 1997

Fasick, Adele
Managing Children's Services in the Public Library, 2nd ed.
Libraries Unlimited, 1998

Fiore, Carole D.
Running Summer Library Reading Programs
Neal-Schuman, 1998

Fraley, Ruth (ed.); Katz, Bill (ed.)
Reference Services for Children and Young Adults
Haworth Press, 1983

Freeman, Judy
Books Kids Will Sit Still For: The Complete Read-Aloud Guide,
2nd ed.
Bowker, 1990

Gillespie, John T. (ed.)
Best Books for Children; Preschool through the Middle Grades, 6th ed.
Bowker, 1998

Horning, Kathleen
From Cover to Cover: Evaluating and Reviewing Children's Books
HarperCollins, 1997

Lima, Carolyn; Lima, John
A To Zoo: Subject Access to Children's Picture Books, 5th ed.
Bowker, 1998

Littlejohn, Carol
Talk That Book: Booktalks That Promote Reading
Linworth, 1999

Moran, Irene (compiler)
Prepare! The Library Public Relations Recipe Book
ALA, 1978

Oppenheim, Joanne; Brenner, Barbara; Boegehold, Betty
Choosing Books For Kids
Ballentine, 1986
How to choose the right book for the right child at the right time.

Reichman, Henry
Censorship and Selection; Issues and Answers for Schools
ALA/AASL, 1993

Saricks, Joyce G.; Brown, Nancy
Reader's Advisory Service in the Public Library
ALA, 1997
Indepth how-to, but geared for helping adults.

Self-Assessment Guide for Children's Services, 2nd ed.
ALA Continuing Library Education Network & Exchange Roundtable, 1994

Smith, Henrietta
Coretta Scott King Awards Book 1970-1999
ALA, 1999
From vision to reality.

Starkel, Kathleen; Fellows, Mary; Nespecca, Sue McCleaf
Youth Services Librarians As Managers
ALA, 1995
A how-to guide from budgeting to personnel.

Thomas, Rebecca
Primary Plots: A Booktalk Guide for Use with Readers Ages Four through Eight
Bowker, 1989

Trelease, Jim
New Read-Aloud Handbook
Penguin, 1989

Vaillancourt, Renee
Bare Bones Young Adult Services: Tips For The Public Library Generalist
ALA, 2000

Van Orden, Phyllis
Library Service to Children
ALA, 1992
> A guide to the research, planning, and policy literature.

Wilson, George; Moss, Joyce
Books for Children to Read Alone: A Guide for Parents and Librarians
Bowker, 1988

Yonkers Public Library
Guide to Subjects and Concepts in Picture Book Format, 2nd ed.
Oceana Publications, 1979
> Rather dated now but still useful to be reminded of old favorites still on library shelves.

Policies and Procedures

Arant, Wendy (ed. 1)
Library Outreach, Partnerships, and Distance Education
Haworth Press, 2000

Children and the Internet: Guidelines for Developing Public Library Policy
ALA, 1998

Minkel, Walter; Feldman, Roxanne Hsu
Delivering Web Reference Services to Young People
ALA, 1998

Unattended Children in the Public Library: A Resource Guide
ALA, 2000

Walter, Virginia
Children and Libraries: Getting It Right
ALA, 2001

Weingand, Darlene E.
Customer Service Excellence: A Concise Guide for Librarians
ALA, 1997

Willis, Mark
Dealing with Difficult People in the Library
ALA, 1999

Children's Web Site Resources

ALSC Cool Sites for Kids
http://www.ala.org/alsc/
children_links.html

*The Librarian's Guide to
Cyberspace for Parents & Kids*
http://www.ala.org/parentspage/
greatsites/guide.html

Kids Zone
http://www.lycoszone.com

*700+ Great Sites: Amazing,
Spectacular, Mysterious,
Wonderful Web Sites for Kids
and the Adults Who Care about
Them*
http://www.ala.org/parentspage/
greatsites/700+/amazing.html

INDEX

ANITRA STEELE has been the Children's Specialist at the Mid-Continent Public Library in Independence, Missouri, since 1976. The first to hold this position, she has developed it to provide programming support and present in-service education classes for the staff members of the library's twenty-nine branches. She also coordinates a large summer reading program and performs "single person" puppet shows.

Active within the state and the Association for Library Service to Children (ALSC), Steele is past chair and continues to serve on the Missouri Youth Summer Library Program Committee. She has served on several in-state children's choice book award committees, numerous ALSC committees, and the ALSC Board. She has taught managing children's services as an adjunct professor and written a column on children's services issues for the *Wilson Library Bulletin.* She also wrote an essay on international children's books in the ninth edition of *Children and Books* (Longman, 1997).